TAMASIN'S WEEKEND FOOD

TAMASIN'S WEEKEND FOOD

Cooking to come home to

Tamasin Day-Lewis

Photography by David Loftus

WEIDENFELD & NICOLSON

CONTENTS

Introduction 6

Friday night 8

Saturday morning 34

Saturday lunch 48

Tea time 72

Saturday supper 86

Sunday lunch 116

Index 142

'If you need to rediscover the pleasures of weekend cooking I hope this book will do it for you… It should suit your every mood from the taxed and harassed what-shall-I-cook tomorrow to instant I-want-it-now gratification, to what can I cook tonight, eat tomorrow, rehash the next day. The weekend starts here.'

Tamasin Day-Lewis

It's Friday morning. The brain is already drifting weekendwards. All the signs are there. Concentration lapsing religiously. Irreligiously. Hedonistic thoughts of fun and food, friends and family and… the sheer stress of it all. The weekend should feel like a holiday, not like an imposed colossus of time off that is really more hard work than hard work. So what to do, what to cook, how to cook, who to eat?

The weekend defines one's style of cooking and eating more than any other time of the week, for all the obvious reasons. Yet the weekend is obstinately full of contradictions. You have time, but you are tired. You have no time – you are tired. You have invited more people than you meant to or you have nowhere to go and nobody to come – YET. You have more time to cook than at any other time of the week, but you don't want to feel you've got to do it – that stops the pleasure of the planning, the mulling, the weekend being the weekend.

Then there is shopping, that most emotive of verbs; food shopping, that most aerobic of spending and deciding exercises. Food shopping says more about our taste than any other kind of shopping. It is not about investments, savings, bargains, it is about pleasure, treats, NOW. And about how we feel about our family, our friends, their tastes, our desire to please them, entice them, seduce them, delight them.

There is destination food shopping at farmers' markets and delis and the impersonal aisle trawling of the supermarket. Whether you do one or the other or both there is still a pleasure/pain principle at work in the tedium of putting everything away when you get back, of filling the fridge like a frigate, finding you already had what you've just bought, not finding enough room for everything, wishing you had a shopper, a packer, a putter-away.

You want simple, easy, fabulous Saturday lunch food, the kind of goodies where provenance is all, which you can just unwrap, peel, dress and adorn the table with. Yet on Saturday afternoon you might want to pore over some byzantine recipe that you have read and reread hungrily, obsessively, for months, seasons, years. You want to laze on Sunday morning but turn out a spectacularly wonderful, traditional, all-the-trimmings Sunday lunch, without having lost a sybaritic second of the morning. Friday night, that longed for semi-colon to the week, is where the weekend starts, full of anticipation and promise, full of exhaustion, the longing for a good drink, a magical dinner, TIME, someone else to take over.

We wrestle anew with these contradictions every week and there is no answer. Every weekend is different – the mood, the season, the guests, the recipes. Things are more structured when we have tiny children; less structured and less predictable when we have teenagers, who will commit to nothing but sleep – other than large quantities of food at strangely different times to the rest of the family. And they certainly won't commit to numbers. So we anticipate, we brook change, we adapt, we stock up, we cook for all eventualities. Therein, in its curiously maddening way, lies the pleasure, in the very uncertainty, in the fact that that is what is expected of us. We are seen as ultimately competent, always happy to dish up food for twelve from ingredients bought for four, as a place where everyone wants to come and eat, drink, enjoy. And if they enjoy, so do we. And in so doing, we have a great weekend.

I have now made two television series which reflect, if not entirely accurately, both a lifestyle I didn't know I possessed and – more accurately – what my family and friends expect of me. The fact that we had to shoot both series through weeks as well as weekends doesn't alter the reality of how I cook for friends and family, the demands of the children, the unexpected guests. There is also the simple pleasure of cooking alongside a cook whose cooking you really know and love. Top of my list for the latter, other than my children and The American, are my friend George, my cousin Deborah and Michelin-starred Irish chef Richard Corrigan. All three are as intrinsic to my cooking life as my best pots and pans. Finding a cooking partner is as dangerous as marriage, but when you find someone simpatico who isn't merely your galley slave but comes with a fully paid up set of skills and a lexicon of their own recipes, you've got it made. These are your best weekend guests, as long as their clearing up is as thorough and inspirational as their culinary talent. Then the weekend ceases to be work at all and becomes fun – all about conspiratorial greed, experimentation and the rediscovery of all the reasons why you love cooking as much as eating. It is an oasis, a break from the lonely grind of everyday menu planning, shopping and cooking. Even that strange, sad, somewhat dislocated time on a Sunday night, before the reality check of Monday morning, loses its peculiar grip as you bask in the afterglow of one weekend and start planning the next.

If you think you've seen some of these recipes before, you're right. My television series anthologized recipes from my past four books. But don't feel cheated – there are plenty of new ones and many have been revised!

If you needed to rediscover the pleasures of weekend cooking, I hope this book will do it for you, but don't just think of it as a Friday to Monday book. It's more about an attitude to food and cooking than about weekending. It should suit your every mood from the taxed and harassed what-shall-I-cook tomorrow to instant I-want-it-now gratification, to what can I cook tonight, eat tomorrow, rehash the next day. The weekend starts here.

TAMASIN DAY-LEWIS

1

Friday night

You have either achieved Everestian heights and completed the weekend shop, wanting nothing more than to slump with a good bottle and an easy, delicious dinner, or you have to raid the store cupboard to find something nurturing to cook. If it's Friday it must be fish or pasta or something slow cooked that you set simmering a day or two ago in anticipation of the descending guests or simply your own end-of-week exhaustion.

SICILIAN PEPPERS

This Sicilian dish is great as a starter or a main course, or it can accompany game or cold roast meat with brio. Make it in advance, and eat it warm or cold.

Serves 4

4 red peppers
1 onion, finely sliced
2 cloves of garlic, chopped
½ an organic vegetable bouillon cube
3 tbsp best extra virgin olive oil
2 tbsp best balsamic vinegar, and by that, I mean an aged, velvety black number that is mellow rather than sharp. Mine is a 20-year-old.
a small bunch of fresh oregano
18 best glossy black olives, halved and stoned
2 salted anchovies, rinsed and boned, or 4 anchovy fillets in olive oil
1½ tbsp salted capers rinsed under a cold tap
sea salt and black pepper

Grill or char your peppers until they are uniformly blackened and softened. Leave them to cool, then the skins should peel away easily. Cut the prepared peppers into long strips.

Cook the onion, garlic and olive oil gently in a covered pan, with a bit of salt and a couple of tablespoons of water. You want the onion to be softened to a purée. Remove the lid, and carry on cooking until the onion is golden, which will take about 40 minutes. Add the strips of pepper, the crumbled bouillon cube and the balsamic vinegar. Cook uncovered for a further 30 minutes, stirring occasionally. You can always add an extra tablespoon or two of water if the mixture seems to be drying out.

Add all the other ingredients, and carry on slow cooking for 20 minutes at a very low temperature; anything more and the anchovies will turn bitter.

Serve the peppers warm or at room temperature with good crusty bread, or with game or cold roast meat as above.

SPICED CHICKEN LIVERS

This is one of the simplest and most delicious titbits of a dish that I have ever cooked. It should be eaten straight from a communal plate, or even the frying pan, your fingers oozing the pinkly sticky, spicy juices, while you clutch a cold glass of something good with your free hand.

Serves 6 as a starter with drinks, depending on greed and what's to follow

450g/1lb organic chicken livers. I'm afraid I take a purist line here – only organic will do, since chemical residues collect in the liver and kidneys.
1½ heaped tsp cumin seeds
1 tsp coriander seeds
1 tsp sea salt crystals
1 tsp black peppercorns
the tip of a tsp of cayenne
1–1½ tbsp plain flour
olive oil or a good-sized knob of unsalted butter

Temper the cumin and coriander in a small frying pan over a gentle heat for 30 seconds to a minute, until the spices exude their scent. Tip into a mortar and crush with the sea salt and peppercorns. Add the cayenne, then the flour, and stir well together. Set aside.

Clean and de-vein the livers, keeping them whole, and removing any green patches. Pat them dry and keep in the fridge until about 30 minutes before you want to cook them.

Just before cooking, roll each liver in the spice mixture in the mortar and put on a plate. Heat a good knob of unsalted butter or olive oil, whichever you prefer, in a frying pan – I come down on the side of butter, with a tiny addition of oil to discourage burning. Throw in the livers when the fat is hot. Allow one side to spit and crisp for a couple of minutes, turn over and repeat, then test with a knife point. When gorgeously oozily pink, shunt the contents of the pan on to a white plate and consume.

INNES BUTTONS
WITH TOASTED HAZELNUTS AND HAZELNUT OIL

How difficult is it to produce perfect lemony, fudgy, lactic little buttons of fresh goat's cheese? Well in England they are a rarity. These examples were the overall winners at the British Cheese Awards in 2002 when I was one of the judges. Order them from The Fine Cheese Company on 01225 448748.

Innes Button cheeses, one per person
endives or treviso
hazelnuts, roasted and crushed
hazelnut oil
black pepper

Innes Button cheeses are best served with some treviso or endives underneath. Add a judicious sprinkling of crushed roasted hazelnuts over each button, a slug of hazelnut oil and a scrunch of pepper.

BAGNA CAUDA

This 'hot bath' of a sauce is garlicky, salt with anchovy and the perfect thing to pass round warm with a selection of crisp raw vegetables and a glass of wine. Fennel, cardoons, carrots, radishes, celery and peppers work well, though sometimes cooked potatoes are used.

Serves 4–6

55g/2oz butter
4 cloves of garlic, peeled and
  very finely sliced
5 salted anchovies, rinsed and
  boned, or 10 anchovy fillets
  in olive oil
200ml/7fl oz olive oil
salt

Melt the butter in a small, deep earthenware pot or in a very heavy-based saucepan over the lowest possible heat. As soon as the butter has melted, add the garlic and sauté for a few seconds. The garlic should not colour. Add the anchovies to the pot and pour in the oil very gradually, stirring all the time. Cook for about 10 minutes on the lowest possible heat, stirring constantly. The dip is ready when the ingredients are well blended and smooth. Season if necessary and serve.

The sauce must be kept hot, which the Piedmontese do in an earthenware pot over a spirit lamp. Special bagna cauda pots are available.

LAYERED PANCAKES
WITH TOMATO SAUCE

This recipe is the kind of assembly job that lasagne is, a layer by layer dish, but has the advantage of your being able to make the tomato sauce and the pancakes a day or two in advance, before building them up, stratum by stratum like a savoury cake. You sprinkle mozzarella and fresh Parmesan cheese between the leaves, before baking the dish like a pasta gratin. Only it isn't pasta, it is layers of soft pancakes bubbling with tomatoey oily juices and oozing fresh mozzarella. My children were as impressed as I was the first time I made it, and I then went on to experiment further with a creamy pesto sauce. A substantial and unusual dish, beautiful enough for a party.

Serves 4

Pancakes
110g/4oz flour
salt
2 eggs
290ml/10fl oz milk
a tiny knob of butter

Tomato sauce
about 1kg/2¼lb tomatoes,
   peeled seeded and
   chopped
1 onion, chopped
2 sticks of celery, chopped
2 cloves of garlic, chopped
1 bay leaf
1 teaspoon each of molasses
   sugar and tomato purée
a splash of red wine
   (optional)

Béchamel sauce
425ml/15fl oz full cream milk
45g/1½oz butter
45g/1½oz flour
grated nutmeg
salt and pepper

PANCAKES

This recipe makes thicker pancakes than you would normally have, but you may add a bit more milk if the batter feels really thick. Leave the batter to rest for 30 minutes and then whisk again. Heat a tiny knob of butter in a heavy pan, pour in a small ladle of batter, and wait until it begins to bronze and bubble before flipping. When the pancake is done, place it on a plate with a palate knife and repeat. For some inexplicable reason, the first pancake doesn't usually work. You should get eight good-sized pancakes from this amount of batter.

TOMATO SAUCE

Sweat the chopped onion in some olive oil. Add the skinned, seeded and chopped tomatoes, celery, chopped garlic and bay leaf, then stir in the molasses sugar and tomato purée. Cook the whole lot down for at least 30 minutes until reduced, thickened and jammy. You can add a splosh of red wine when you add the tomatoes if you like. Pass your tomato sauce through the coarse disc of the mouli if you prefer your sauce less textured. Use tinned tomatoes if it is not the time of year for good fresh tomatoes.

BÉCHAMEL SAUCE

Heat the milk. Melt the butter in a saucepan. Add the plain flour, cook for a few minutes, then stir in the hot milk. Cook the béchamel for at least 20 minutes so that it no longer smells floury. Season with grated nutmeg, salt and pepper.

Assembly

2 fresh mozzarella di bufala, chopped into small dice

4 tbsp fresh Parmesan cheese, grated

a handful of fresh basil, chopped

ASSEMBLING THE DISH

Once you have made the tomato and béchamel sauces and the pancakes, you are ready to assemble the dish.

Preheat the oven to 180°C/350°F/Gas 4. Stir the tomato sauce into the béchamel. Butter a gratin dish, place a pancake on the bottom and spread a thin layer of the tomato and béchamel sauces over the top. Sprinkle with mozzarella, Parmesan, basil, salt and pepper and cover with another pancake. Continue layering the pancakes until you have a sort of leaning tower of Pisa, eight pancake-storeys high. The top must be sauce, Parmesan, basil, salt and pepper, not mozzarella, which would turn to goo.

Cover the dish with a sheet of greased greaseproof paper and bake for about 20 minutes. Remove the greaseproof and continue to cook for a further 10 minutes until bubbling and gorgeous. Leave it to stand outside the oven before you cut it into triangular wedges just like a cake. Serve with a plain green salad. This is substantial with a capital S!

LAYERED PANCAKES
WITH PESTO SAUCE

There are three things you need to remember for this recipe. First, use fresh pesto. Second, don't add more than three tablespoons of it to the béchamel for this quantity of ingredients and people – it is extremely rich and olive oily. Third, if you add the pesto to the béchamel when the sauce has already begun to cool down, it will keep its magical brilliant green hue and not turn muddy khaki. I am not sure why, since once it goes into the oven it is going to be cooked. I can only imagine the layers of sauce and pancake somehow protect it.

Serves 4

Pesto sauce
2 handfuls of fresh basil leaves
30g/1oz pine nuts
1 clove of garlic, crushed
120ml/4fl oz olive oil
1 tsp sea salt
30g/1oz Parmesan cheese,
  grated

Pancakes
110g/4oz flour
salt
2 eggs
290ml/10fl oz milk
a tiny knob of butter

Béchamel sauce
425ml/15fl oz full cream milk
45g/1½oz butter
45g/1½oz flour
grated nutmeg
salt and pepper

Make the pesto by grinding the basil, pine nuts, garlic, olive oil and salt in a pestle and mortar, or whizz everything to a paste in a food processor. Either way, stir in the Parmesan afterwards.

Make the pancakes and béchamel and assemble the dish as described on page 16–17, adding pesto instead of tomato sauce to the béchamel.

This is a great vegetarian party dish. You can, of course, make your fresh pesto in advance and keep it in the fridge under a layer of olive oil that you then stir back into it when you are ready to use it. This time, try a tomato salad as a side dish, rather than an all-green feast.

STUFFED CABBAGE
IN THE TROO STYLE

If the recipe hadn't been Jane Grigson's, I'm pretty sure I wouldn't have stopped, looked and cooked; after all, what is so special about sausages and cabbage? And just how effective can the alchemy of the two be, to transmute them into something so far from what the imagination can conceive of? The answer is, good enough for me to have cooked this dish several times each winter for nearly two decades. The two simple elements transcend their original state and unify so flawlessly that they want for nothing more; no extra can improve them. The long, slow cooking of the cabbage, leaching its intense juices into the finest organic Swaddles Green pork sausages, which in turn exude their fat to coat and intensify the flavour of the cabbage, with only the addition of butter, salt and pepper, is a process of stunning simplicity. The pink and green strata compact almost into a loaf or torte, and the whole, served with its copious juice, wants only for a baked potato, some coarsely bashed carrot and swede, and a trekker's appetite. Never a problem.

Serves 4

1.4–2kg/3–4½lb cabbage, Savoy or Dutch
675g/1½lb best organic plain pork sausages, Swaddles Green make theirs with no nitrites (order on 01460 234387)
salt, pepper, butter

Preheat the oven to 150°C/300°F/Gas 2. Shred the cabbage into thin strips, coring it first, and blanch it in a huge vat of boiling, salted water for five minutes. Drain it in a colander and run the cold tap over it to prevent further cooking at this stage. Butter an ovenproof pot.

Slit the sausage skins and push out all the sausage meat on to a plate, discarding the skins. Place a third of the cabbage in the bottom of the pot and season. Place half the sausage meat in a layer over the cabbage. Continue with a layer of cabbage and sausage, finishing with a layer of cabbage, seasoning each layer as you go, and dotting the top with butter. Cover tightly with a layer of greaseproof and a lid, and cook in the oven for 2–2½ hours. I have served the children at seven o'clock, then reheated the dish for half an hour later in the evening and it came to no grief at all.

LASAGNE AL FORNO

I had been minding my own business and making this classic dish in my own way for years before I came across Marcella Hazan's version. I am writing this in the hope that if you don't know it already, I might be able to convince you of its infinite superiority. A ragu is characterized by its mellow, gentle flavour, so don't blanch at the idea of adding milk to the meat first, it protects the meat from the acidic bite of the tomatoes you will add later. Remember to add salt to the meat as soon as you start cooking it, to leech the juice from the meat for the sauce, and do not think that lean mince is the answer. It ain't. You need a good marbling of fat for a sweeter ragu.

Serves 8

1kg/2¼lb ground beef chuck, or similar, with plenty of fat. You can add ⅓ part ground pork to the beef if you wish
2 boxes dried lasagne, you will probably need 1⅓ boxes, of the sort that needs no precooking
2–3 tbsp olive oil
a knob of butter
2 large onions, finely chopped
3 sticks celery, chopped
3 carrots, finely diced
3 or 4 cloves of garlic, finely chopped
salt and fresh black pepper
2 bay leaves
240ml/8fl oz milk
nutmeg
240ml/8fl oz white wine
1 x 400–450g/13–16oz tin of plum tomatoes
freshly grated Parmesan cheese
1.2 litre/2 pints of béchamel, made with a bay leaf and nutmeg (see page 16)

Preheat the oven to 200°C/400°F/Gas 6. Warm the oil and butter in a heavy cast-iron pot, add the onion, and sauté gently until softened and translucent. Add the celery, carrots and garlic, cook for another couple of minutes, stirring to coat well. Add the ground beef and a large pinch of salt, and grind over some pepper. Stir until the beef has lost its raw pink look. Add the bay leaves and milk, and simmer gently for about 10 minutes, until the meat has absorbed the milk. Add a suspicion of nutmeg, about ⅓ teaspoon. Add the wine, and let it simmer until it has evaporated, then add the cut-up tomatoes with their juice and stir thoroughly.

Cook at a lazy simmer, with just an intermittent bubble breaking through the surface, uncovered, for three hours or more. The fat will have separated from the sauce, but it will not be dry. Taste, and correct the seasoning.

Pour just enough béchamel to cover the base of your greased baking dish, then add a layer of lasagne, followed by a layer of the ragu, a layer of béchamel, and a good handful of Parmesan. Continue with two or three more layers, until your sauces are both used up, add a final sprinkling of Parmesan, and bake in the oven for about 30 minutes. The dish should be bubbling all over, and the knife should slip easily through the layers of lasagne.

This ragu is also great with spaghetti or tagliatelli, and makes a brilliant cottage pie.

PASTA PUTTANESCA

This has to be one of the greatest store-cupboard dishes of my cooking life, its flagrant spiciness responsible for its soubriquet, 'tart's pasta'. I always have tins of plum tomatoes, anchovies, Seggiano olive paste, anchovies, salted capers, dried or fresh chillies and pasta in the house. Nothing could be simpler, more warming or more delicious.

Serves 4

450g/1lb spaghetti, penne or
    other pasta
1 large onion, peeled and
    finely chopped
olive oil
4 cloves of garlic, peeled and
    finely sliced
1 red chilli, seeded and finely
    chopped
2 × 400–450g/13–16oz tins
    whole plum tomatoes
1 tbsp good black olive paste
a tin of anchovies in olive oil,
    drained
a handful of salted capers,
    rinsed under running water
24 olives, a mix of fruity black,
    green and Niçoise, pitted
    and halved
Tabasco or cayenne pepper
    (optional)
a handful of chopped flat-leaf
    parsley

Sauté the onion gently in a couple of tablespoons of olive oil until it is starting to soften, then add the garlic and cook until both are translucent and soft.

Add the chilli and cook a little longer before adding the tomatoes, cutting them into the pan and stirring. Allow the juices to run and then cook until the sauce has started to thicken, but do not let all the juice bubble away. This takes about 15 minutes. Meanwhile, start cooking the pasta according to the instructions on the packet.

Stir the olive paste into the sauce and add the chopped anchovies, which will melt in quickly, with the capers and olives. You will not need salt – the anchovies and capers are quite salty enough. Taste for seasoning – if the dish is not hot enough, you can add some Tabasco or cayenne pepper.

Amalgamate for three or four minutes, then turn the sauce into the drained pasta which you have put back in the pan with a little of its cooking water and a knob of butter. Add the parsley and serve from the pot.

WINTER PASTICCIO

I used red onions, leeks and cherry tomatoes in this delicious dish of penne baked with roasted vegetables. I added a white globe of Pannarello, a cheese that melted like butter into the pasta and was sharp and strong in equal measure. You can also use Fontina, and, since it doesn't turn quite so liquid, a couple of spoonfuls of mascarpone. Lubricance is what you're after.

Serves 4

4 medium red onions, peeled and quartered
4 fat leeks, the whites only, peeled and cut into 4cm/1½in barrels
2 courgettes, cut into 2.5cm/1in chunks
1 bulb fennel, ruthlessly stripped to its firm heart and quartered
2 × 200g/7oz packets of organic cherry tomatoes
olive oil
2–3 sprigs of thyme
salt and pepper
340g/12oz organic penne pasta
6 slices prosciutto or culatello
6 anchovies
a clove of garlic
a handful of basil leaves
170g/6oz Pannarello or Fontina cheese cut into dice
2 tbsp mascarpone

Preheat the oven to 190°C/375°F/Gas 5. Put the vegetables on a roasting tray and dribble on olive oil, rolling them around to cover. Scatter on the thyme, salt and pepper, and put in the oven until roasted and softened, about 30 minutes. Keep the leeks well bathed in oil so they don't brown.

Cook the penne until al dente in plenty of fast-boiling salted water. Put the torn prosciutto, anchovies, garlic and basil in the food processor with 2–4 tablespoons of olive oil and blitz briefly. You want a coarse-textured gunge rather than a sludge! Turn the contents of the bowl into the drained pasta, add the vegetables, the Pannarello or Fontina and the mascarpone and amalgamate well; grind on some more black pepper. Turn into a greased gratin dish, and bake for 20 minutes. You can sprinkle the pasticcio with flat-leaf parsley to serve and offer Parmesan if you wish, but it is delicious as is with a plainly dressed salad.

BAKED COD
WITH ROMESCO SAUCE AND GREEK POTATOES

Here is a dish that wouldn't shame your smartest dinner. I take a sort of perverse pride in wowing people with dishes that use the very best ingredients transformed through the alchemy of the stove, yet are almost ludicrously easy in their execution. You could offer a bowl of home-made romesco sauce if you like, it works wonderfully well with white fish.

Serves 4

Greek potatoes

1kg/2¼lb potatoes, cut long
    and thin into about 4 pieces
    if they are medium sized
225g/8oz onion, peeled and
    finely chopped
6 cloves of garlic
a handful fresh thyme or
    oregano
salt and black pepper
290ml/10fl oz best olive oil
the juice of 2 lemons

Baked cod

1 thick fillet of really fresh cod,
    about 1 kg/2¼lb, and by thick,
    I mean 2.5–4cm/1–1½ in
olive oil
sea salt and black pepper

Romesco sauce

30g/1oz whole blanched
    almonds
30g/1oz whole roasted
    hazelnuts
225g/8oz skinned and seeded
    tomatoes, or the equivalent
    from a tin, with juice
2 cloves of garlic, finely
    chopped
6 tbsp best olive oil
a slice of stale bread, brown
    or white
2 tbsp red wine vinegar
4 tbsp fino sherry
1 red chilli, seeded and finely
    chopped, or cayenne to taste

Preheat the oven to 200°C/400°F/Gas 6. Put the peeled and sliced potatoes into a gratin dish or roasting tin so that they fit snugly in one layer. Throw in the onion and garlic and the herbs stripped from their stems, season and add the olive oil and lemon juice. Now add enough water barely to cover. Cook for 45 minutes before turning the potatoes over and cooking for another 45 minutes. An hour and a half should do it. Cook your fish during the last 15 minutes.

Butter a gratin dish thickly and lay your cod to rest in it, skin side down. Dribble some really fine olive oil over the top, Ravida or Seggiano if possible. Season well. Bake for 15 minutes, then test with the point of a sharp knife or skewer. If it goes right through the flesh with ease and no resistance, the fish is done.

ROMESCO SAUCE

Roast the almonds briefly in a moderate oven until pale gold. Heat four tablespoons of the olive oil slowly in a pan, with the chopped garlic. When it is hot, remove and reserve the garlic and fry the bread briefly on both sides until crisp and golden. Remove from the pan, add two more tablespoons of oil and then the tomatoes and chilli, stirring until it is reduced and jammily thickened. About 10–15 minutes. Grind the nuts in a food processor, or in a mortar for a better texture, then add the bread and garlic and continue to pound with the vinegar and sherry. Stir in the cooled tomato sauce and serve in the mortar.

COD CHARMOULA

A charmoula is a feisty Moroccan spice rub, which lends itself well to fish, chicken, lamb or pork, so play around accordingly. If you can slash the skin of the fish, flesh or fowl and maximize penetration, so much the better.

Serves 4

1kg/2¼lb cod fillet, cut
  2.5cm/1in thick
1 tsp cumin seeds
1 tsp coriander seeds
1 onion
3 cloves of garlic
a bunch each of flat-leaf
  parsley and coriander
1 tsp paprika
½ tsp dried root ginger
12 glossy black olives, stoned
1 preserved lemon
4 tbsp olive oil
salt, pepper, cayenne

Temper the cumin and coriander seeds in a small frying pan over a medium heat briefly, and by that, I mean until you smell toasted spice and they begin to brown, 30–60 seconds. Then pound them together in a mortar. Peel and chop the onion and garlic, then put them into a food processor with the ground spices, herbs, paprika and ginger. Blitz until they look finely chopped. Chop the olives and lemon more coarsely, and stir them into the mixture, then stir in a bit of olive oil to slacken the mixture further to a paste. Season to taste with salt, pepper and cayenne.

Slap the paste all over the cod, down into the slashes, cover with clingfilm and place in the fridge for at least two hours, but overnight if you can.

Remove from the fridge and bring back to room temperature before cooking. Preheat the oven to 200°C/400°F/Gas 6. Place the cod in a roasting tin, and cook for about 20 minutes. Check with a skewer to make sure the fish is not still resistant.

If you like, accompany with a bowl of sheep's or Greek yoghurt thinned with a spoonful of milk, into which you have stirred a teaspoon of tempered cumin seeds and some fresh, finely chopped coriander, salt and pepper. I serve this dish with steamed couscous. Feel free to add roasted, skinned red peppers and any other roasted vegetables you like to the couscous.

SALMON FISHCAKES
WITH CRÈME FRAÎCHE TARTARE

When I was a child it seemed extraordinarily glamorous to eat salmon fishcakes for breakfast, but that is what my grandfather did, sitting at the head of an immaculately gleaming 18th-century oak refectory table. For a special treat, Rhoda, my grandmother's cook, would make a couple for me too. They are still a treat, and will always remain so. I would not, however, be interested in eating them if they were made with farmed salmon. Salmon fishcakes should be made with the leftovers from a perfectly moist, wild salmon whose flesh has slightly gelled overnight, been flaked but not crushed to a pulp, and bound with some dry, smooth, unbuttery mashed potato and a healthy seasoning of chopped flat-leaf parsley, coarsely ground pepper and sea salt.

Serves 6

about 560g/1¼lb wild salmon, cooked
about 310g/11oz cooked potato, mashed without milk and butter, but even half and half salmon and potato works if that is the quantity of fish you have left
a handful of flat-leaf parsley, chopped
sea salt and freshly ground black pepper
2 eggs, beaten
85g/3oz stale wholemeal bread, baked in small squares in a slow oven to dry out for 15 minutes, then whizzed to crumbs
vegetable or olive oil for frying

Mash the salmon into the potato roughly, so it still has coarse-textured flakes and is not a homogenous purée. Season and throw in the parsley, then shape the mixture into 2.5cm/1in thick cakes and place them on a large flat plate. Keep covered in the fridge for an hour or two to firm up, or longer if it is convenient.

Whisk the eggs on one large flat plate, and spread the dried breadcrumbs on another. Dip the fishcakes first into the egg on both sides, then turn them in the breadcrumbs, making sure the sides are well crumbed too. Place them on a third large plate. Heat a shallow film of oil, about 60ml/2fl oz, in a frying pan over a medium heat. Put the fishcakes in and fry for four minutes or so a side until golden brown. Drain on kitchen paper and serve, two per person, with a dollop of crème fraîche tartare.

CRÈME FRAÎCHE TARTARE

This is a lighter tartare than the classic, but every bit as moreish; the sort of thing you have to dip your finger into, or scrape round the plate when you think no one is looking. It works well with white fish as well as fishcakes. Curiously, it appeals to children, too – the usual version does not in my experience.

1 organic egg yolk
1 tsp Dijon mustard
sea salt
Tabasco
3–4 tbsp crème fraîche,
  d'Isigny is one of the best
2 tsp tarragon vinegar
1 tsp tarragon, chopped
1 heaped tbsp flat-leaf
  parsley, chopped
1 tsp chives, chopped
1 tbsp rinsed capers, chopped
1 tbsp finely chopped
  cornichons

Beat the egg yolk with the mustard, sea salt and a few dashes of Tabasco until emulsified. Add the crème fraîche, a spoonful at a time, and one teaspoon of the tarragon vinegar, whisking well with a small balloon whisk. Whisk until thick, but pourable. Stir in the other ingredients with the second teaspoon of vinegar. Adjust the seasoning.

BREAST OF LAMB COOKED IN THE DAUBE STYLE

This is, without doubt, one of the best dishes I have ever cooked. I used two whole breasts as we were eight, and each weighed about 1.4kg / 3lb. Having abandoned this dish for three hours, I could smell its winey depths several rooms away when I came to take it out of the oven. A sweetly flavoured meat that you could cut with a spoon after its long, slow cooking.

Serves 8

2 x 1.4kg/3lb whole breasts of lamb on the bone
5 rashers oak-smoked bacon, snipped into 1cm/½in pieces
5 large carrots cut in 1cm/½in dice
4 sticks celery, chopped
2 onions, chopped
6 cloves of garlic
rosemary, bay and parsley stalks tied together with string
1 bottle good red wine
2 x 400g/13oz tins tomatoes
olive oil, salt and pepper

Put the snipped rashers in a large, heavy-bottomed casserole and heat gently until the fat begins to run. Throw in the carrots, celery, onions and garlic, and sprinkle with a tablespoon or two of olive oil.

Tuck the breasts in next to each other in the casserole, with the bouquet under the flap of one. Season. Heat the wine to boiling point, set light to it, and watch carefully until the flames die down. Pour it over the meat. Add the tomatoes, chopping and sinking them into the wine as you go.

Put a layer of greaseproof paper over the top of the pot, cover it with the lid, and cook in a coolish oven, 150°C/300°F/Gas 2 for three hours.

Remove the casserole dish, unlid it and, with a bulb baster, remove the liquid, tomato-coloured fat as far as you dare. I skimmed off 300ml/10½fl oz. Don't carve the meat conventionally – it will be so tender that you can cut right through to the bottom in chunks for each portion. Scoop out the vegetables and bacon with the juices, and anoint the meat with them. Is there anything as good as buttery mashed potato with a dish like this?

PORK HOCK AND BEAN CASSEROLE

This is one of those deep-down, earthy dishes with the treacly blackness of the molasses and star anise underscoring its meaty juices. I used Swaddles Green (01460 234387) organic pork hocks which cooked down to a gluey, falling-off-the-bone sweetness. Add some good sausages if you like.

Serves 6

3 organic pork hocks
500g/1lb 2oz packet of
   haricot or cannellini beans,
   soaked overnight in cold
   water
ham or chicken stock, or
   water to cover
half a jar of Meridian
   blackstrap molasses
170g/6oz molasses sugar
4 tsp English mustard powder
4 large onions, each stuck
   with 3 or 4 cloves
3 star anise
12 white peppercorns

Preheat the oven to 130°C/250°F/Gas ½. Drain the beans and put them in a heavy-bottomed casserole pot with stock or water to cover. Bring to the boil, skim off the scum and simmer for 30 minutes. They will still be hard. Pour off some of the stock, so that the beans are just covered.

Put a ladle or two of the hot stock from the pot into a bowl with the molasses, molasses sugar and mustard powder, and stir well until everything has dissolved. Put the clove-studded onions and star anise into the pot, then the treacly mixture, and bury the hocks in the pot. Add the peppercorns, bring just up to boiling point, then put the pot, covered with a lid, into the bottom of the oven for four hours.

Remove the lid and return to the oven for another hour or so. At this stage you can also bury the best pork sausages you can find in the pot before putting it back in the oven. Serve with mashed potato to mop up the juices.

PORK FILLET EN PAPILLOTE
WITH DIJON, FENNEL AND BLACK OLIVES.

Serves 6–7

1kg/2¼lb pork fillet
2 bulbs fennel, with frondy
   bits
2 red onions
2 sticks celery, with their
   leaves
12 good black olives
olive oil and butter
salt and pepper
a good slug of Pernod,
   say 2 tbsp
2 heaped dsrtsp Dijon
   mustard

Preheat the oven to 180°C/350°F/Gas 4. Slice the pork fillets almost in half lengthwise, then open them out like butterflies and flatten them slightly with your hands.

Trim the bulbs of fennel and onion rigorously to the point of wastefully – you want the tenderest, juiciest parts of both – and chop into a fine duxelles, which means smaller than dice by quite some way. String the sticks of celery and chop as for the fennel and onions.

Stew all the vegetables together in a little olive oil and butter until softened and translucent and season. Add the halved, pitted olives, pour on the Pernod, allow it to bubble briefly, dollop on the mustard, and stir it into the mixture to bind it off the heat. Cool slightly. Spread it in the centre of the pork fillets, then simply press them together, and fix with string, which I tied in a sort of large, raggedy blanket stitch.

Place each fillet on its own bit of foil and seal loosely. Place all the fillets on a flat baking tray, and cook in the oven for 35 minutes. Test with a skewer. In this time, mine were cooked through, with a tinge of pink, and had created a good puddle of juice. Serve with new potatoes and something simple like broad or runner beans, or fresh peas.

HONEY-BLACKENED DUCK LEGS

The mahogany-dark chestnut honey turns to black when you bake these duck legs, and spoonfuls of lumpy bitter marmalade give the dish a sweet-sour taste. Honey used in place of sugar always darkens the food, because the single sugars in it caramelize so readily.

Serves 6

6 organic duck legs
a glass of whatever red wine
  you happen to be drinking

Marinade
2 heaped dsrtsp Seggiano
  chestnut honey
2 dsrtsp chunky bitter
  marmalade
1 tsp star anise, pounded in a
  mortar then sieved
juice of a lime
2 dsrtsp Tamari sauce
8–10 black peppercorns,
  cracked and scrunched a
  little in a mortar

Preheat the oven to 200°C/400°F/Gas 6. Mix the marinade ingredients together in a bowl, stirring well, then pour over the duck legs, and either leave for a couple of hours or cover and put in the fridge overnight.

Place the legs in an earthenware dish, spoon the marinade over evenly, and bake. After 20 minutes turn the legs over, the top side will already be a wonderful molassy colour.

After another 20 minutes, throw the wine into the dish. Scrape all the dark, sticky juices into the wine, and turn the legs for a final 20-minute blast.

I served these duck legs on rice, with purple sprouting broccoli.

OXTAIL STEWED WITH GRAPES

I have been cooking this classic Elizabeth David dish, 'queue de boeuf des vignerons', traditionally cooked during the grape harvest, for years. It is something to prepare the night before so you can skim the fat from the surface before gently heating it through the next day. The sweet succulence of the gluey meat and green grape is wonderfully harmonious, a dish for the autumn and winter.

Serves 6–8

2 oxtails, cut into 5cm/2in lengths (ask your butcher to do this)
100g/3½oz salt pork or unsmoked bacon bought in one piece
2 large onions, chopped
2 large carrots, diced
bouquet of 2 bay leaves, parsley, thyme and 2 crushed cloves of garlic tied in a bunch
a pinch of mace or allspice
salt and pepper
900g/2lb white grapes

Steep the oxtail in cold water for at least two hours so that the blood soaks out. Cut the salt pork or bacon, without the rind, into little cubes. Put them into a heavy cooking pot and add the vegetables on top. Starting on a low heat, cook for 10 minutes until the fat is running from the bacon. Add the pieces of oxtail, and put the bouquet in the centre. Season the meat and add the spices. Cover the pot and cook gently for 20 minutes.

Preheat the oven to 140°C/275°F/Gas 1. Add the grapes, which you have picked off their stalks and crushed lightly in a bowl. Cover the pot with two sheets of greaseproof paper and the lid. Transfer to a very slow oven and cook for at least three hours. Oxtail varies in quality and sometimes takes a good deal longer, and unless the meat is so soft and tender it is almost falling from the bones it will not be good.

Once cooked, quickly transfer the pieces of oxtail and a few of the little bits of bacon to another pot or to a serving dish, and keep them hot while you sieve all the rest of the ingredients through the finest mesh of a mouli-legume. Pour the resulting sauce over the oxtail. Serve with some plain boiled or mashed potatoes.

An alternative method is to cook the dish for a half an hour less, take out the oxtail and leave the sieved sauce separate so that excess fat can be removed from the top when it is cold. Having done this, put the warmed sauce over the meat and heat on top of the stove rather than in the oven. All-round heat tends to make the sauce oily, whereas direct heat will retain its consistency. The dish can be reheated two or three times without damage.

MOUSSE AU CHOCOLAT

A rich delicious mousse with a darkly bitter density. Best made the day before and left in the fridge overnight before serving.

Serves 8–10

140g/5oz vanilla caster sugar
3 whole eggs, separated
3 extra yolks
1 tbsp Green and Black's cocoa powder
200ml/7fl oz double cream
85g/3oz unsalted butter
225g/8oz best bitter chocolate, I used L'Atelier's 70 per cent couverture chocolate
1 tbsp Armagnac or Cognac

Put 55g/2oz of the sugar, all 6 egg yolks, the cocoa powder and the cream in the top of a double saucepan over simmering water. Keep whisking it over a gentle heat until it thickens enough to coat a wooden spoon. Take the top saucepan out of the bottom one, and, off the heat, add small pieces of the butter and chocolate and stir until fully melted. Add the alcohol and stir it in.

Whisk the three egg whites with the rest of the sugar. Add the sugar as you whisk not at the end – this method makes a thickly glossy meringue which you want to whisk to soft peak stage. Fold the meringue lightly into the chocolate mixture, which you have decanted into a bowl. Pour into a large soufflé dish and refrigerate before serving.

WHITE CHOCOLATE TART
WITH RASPBERRIES

I first cooked this tart at the end of October, when there was an unexpected and welcome supply of late Scottish raspberries. It made autumn recede temporarily, and then I couldn't resist cooking it again with my friend Brigid for a Boxing Day lunch party. We'd all been asked to bring a dish, and I happened upon some Third World flown-in berries, which it was worth abandoning seasonal principles for. White tarts are somehow fitting for Christmas food, particularly when the top looks like thick snow. I am not, on the whole, a flavoured-pastry person, but Christmas brings on the aforementioned abandon, and a dark chocolatey crust made with Green and Black's organic cocoa is a delightful exception, and a contrast to the acre of white ice-rink topping it. I dusted the top with cocoa at the last minute.

Serves 6–8

Pastry
110g/4oz plain flour
2 tsp Green and Black's
   organic cocoa powder
1 heaped dsrtsp unrefined
   icing sugar
55g/2oz cold butter, cut into
   small pieces
1 egg yolk

Filling
200ml/7fl oz crème fraîche
240ml/8fl oz double cream
170g/6oz Green and Black's
   organic white chocolate
200g/7oz fresh raspberries

Preheat the oven to 200°C/400°F/Gas 6. Grease a 23cm/9 in tart tin.

For the pastry, sift the flour, cocoa and sugar into the bowl of your food processor, add the cold butter and whizz briefly. Add the egg yolk and a tablespoon or two of ice-cold water, and process again just to the point at which the pastry coheres. Wrap in clingfilm and refrigerate for half an hour. Roll out on some flour sifted with a bit more cocoa and line the tart tin. Bake blind for 20 minutes, then remove the beans and cook for a further 10 minutes. The pastry case should be crisp and browned slightly. Leave to cool.

For the filling, heat the crème fraîche with 100ml/3½fl oz of the double cream. Break the chocolate into a bowl, pour the hot cream over it and leave for a minute, then stir until the chocolate dissolves. Cover with clingfilm with some air holes punched in it, and put in the fridge for two to three hours.

Very lightly crush the raspberries with a fork to let the juice run a little (they should remain whole), and put them in a single layer on the pastry base. Whisk the remaining double cream until thick but still soft, not rigid, and fold it into the chocolate mixture. Smooth this over the raspberry base with a rubber spatula and refrigerate for at least another hour. Eat cold.

2

Saturday morning

A perfect time to start making the loaves you've been promising yourself for weeks that you'd bake, filling the kitchen with the best smells of all — the steamy, yeasty, nutty, wheaty aromas of proper, slow-rise bread. Or try mixing up a quick, fruity, crumble-topped muffin or baking some soda bread — the easiest loaf at all — to eat warm with breakfast.

BREAD

I FIND PRODUCING a home-made loaf at any meal brings about a quite extraordinary reaction. It is not nostalgia exactly, because most of us were not lucky enough to be brought up on home-made bread. But it is nostalgia for what might have been and could obviously be, when the beholder sees the apparent ease with which the warm, yeasted offering is brought to the table as though it were just an ordinary part of the proceedings and of keeping a good table. It sort of makes it seem possible, which I now know it is, without being a slave to it. Home-made bread, toasted, with home-made crab apple or bramble jelly in the autumn and early winter, later followed by Seville orange marmalade – my other new-found skill – is now a habit it would be difficult to break.

Literature on the subject of bread making is so extensive as to be seriously off-putting to the beginner, even when a relatively experienced cook like myself. What you want is a simple, crusted loaf that has a fine texture and flavour, and is not gluey, taut-grained, crumbly, spongy or leaden. You want it to work the first and every subsequent time, instilling confidence, a sense of achievement and the feeling that finally, finally, one has the sort of kitchen that smells how a kitchen should. There is no better scent than that of a fresh, yeasted loaf rising, cooking and cooling before you eat it – still warm, nutty, crusty, with a just-too-large-to-be-decent slab of deliquescent unsalted butter.

It is perfectly possible to fit bread making into the most hectic of schedules, and without being a martyr to the cause. It does not demand the sort of attention that many supposedly simpler dishes do. I can leave it to rise and go out running a.m. or make and eat dinner as it rises p.m. If you bake three loaves at a time and freeze one or two, depending on the size of your family, bread making does not become a chore – it stays a delight. Every bag of flour you buy, albeit the same make as the last one you bought, is different, so you need to feel what you're doing, not just follow instructions. That takes experience, but all the bread I've baked has been far better than supermarket bread, and most of it has been REALLY good. The ambient temperature makes a difference.

Fresh yeast bought at the supermarket bakery counter isn't always fresh. I have been sold dead yeast on a number of occasions. Always inspect the packet before you walk away. If it is pale and crumbly rather than rubbery, and in a homogeneous, springy block, do not accept it. Some recipes say 30g of yeast per 450g loaf, some say 45g per three 450g loaves. I have made both. My son Harry was complaining at the over-yeasty taste of the bread with the larger concentration, when I found a recipe on another packet of flour, which, incidentally, reversed the kneading and knocking-back processes from my original recipe. Less yeast, and kneading after the first mixing rather than the second, work much better, both for texture and taste.

As for the kneading, four or five minutes is not enough. You have to knead vigorously for eight to ten minutes and only then, in my experience, will your loaf not turn into a compressed breezeblock. It is the only hard work throughout the process, and its rigours are both comforting and enjoyable if you are prepared to find them so, which I decidedly am. No bread-making machine or dough hook I've used has done it for me so far, and the dried yeast you use in machines does not produce bread of the taste or texture that you are making home-made bread for in the first place. Circular loaves baked in a low-sided tin work the best, since you get the highest surface area of crisp crust, but don't make a loaf in too big a tin, since the loaf will spread sideways during the rise as well as upwards.

My baking technique advanced dramatically after a highly informative day with master miller John Lister of Shipton Mill in Gloucestershire. It appears that the rise of the commercial loaf, in both senses, is the result of two things. Post-19th century, came the discovery that brewer's yeast could enable the baker to prove the loaf quicker and quicker, using more and more yeast. Then, in the 1950s, came the Chorleywood Bread Process. Bakers discovered that one of the key elements of good bread is putting in energy. 'Kneading is not for fun, it is to condition the dough,' John told me. 'Then came the discovery that there are chemicals which can achieve this in a very short time, you can do the mix in 20 seconds, and that 20 seconds is the equivalent to 11 kilowatt hours of energy. It will prove in minutes, but high-speed bread is totally different to the hand-baked loaf. You are trading time for the mechanical input of energy and chemicals. You can make things bread shaped but they are not bread. The fermentation process is the most important part of bread making. If you remove this process, how can you still call it bread? Imagine if the French took fermentation out of wine making and still called it wine. Fermentation is the critical part, it transforms wheat flours from inedible to edible. If you allow time for the fermentation to happen properly, the bread starts to digest the proteins in the wheat and transform them from indigestible to digestible. People might be put off by having to leave their bread to rise for 24 hours, but you just leave it alone in a warm place and it's ready. Bread NEEDS fermentation, it is the crucial element that changes it from raw to cooked. A long fermentation means the yeast produces sugars, and converts the carbohydrates into sugars so that they can multiply faster, then the sugars caramelize and you get a beautiful coloured crust that you can recognize immediately.'

Not only beautiful to look at, this bread has the texture that no instantly made loaf has, and a crust that you really have to chew. Crisp and crusty, it almost cracks like an egg shell when you cut it. Good bread is also about the wheat the miller buys, the art of blending it, how it comes out slightly toasted from between the millstones in a process that, again, you cannot speed up. 'Every time I try to make things more complex I come back to the simple best four loaves and change the process. Look at Monsieur Poilâne, he only makes one loaf. It's about best wheats, the simplest process and really understanding fermentation. It's a lifetime's work, just focusing on those aspects,' John told me.

So don't expect to achieve instant perfection. Just enjoy, as I do, the mysterious part of the process that is responsible for every batch you bake being wholly unlike the one you last baked. It is eternally fascinating to me how ambient temperature, the amount and age of yeast and flour, the warmth of your hands and the strength you exert that particular day during the kneading, as well as many other things that I am only just beginning to learn to analyse, can affect the finished loaf.

MALTED GRAIN LOAF

Home-made bread, toasted, with home-made crab apple or bramble jelly or Seville orange marmalade is now a breakfast habit it would be hard to break.

Makes 3 loaves
I leave it to you to vary the flavour with the different flours and seeds

1kg/2¼lb Shipton Mill or Dove's Farm organic malted grain flour
500g/1lb 2oz strong organic wholemeal flour, again Shipton Mill or Dove's Farm
3 heaped tsp sea salt
45g/1½oz fresh yeast
3 heaped tsp molasses sugar
850ml/1½ pints hand-hot water; it should feel neither boiling, nor tepid
3 tbsp extra virgin olive oil
sesame, sunflower or poppy seeds and a little milk for the tops of the loaves

Tip the flours out into a very large mixing bowl and add the salt. Boil a kettle, and put about 200ml/7fl oz of boiling water in a measuring jug, topping up to the 425ml/15fl oz mark with water from the cold tap. The water should now feel hand hot. Drop in the molasses sugar and fresh yeast and stir vigorously for a few seconds until the liquid looks creamy. Leave it for 15 minutes to rise. I still find this as absorbing as I did when I baked my first loaf, the living organism fizzing, popping, bubbling, and the sudden rush and rise in volume like a geyser with a will of its own inhabiting the jug.

Pour the contents of the jug into the flour, and then another 425ml/15fl oz of hand-hot water immediately afterwards, then pour in the three tablespoons of olive oil. With one hand, start working the wet dough together until it coheres completely into a ball, then remove it from the bowl on to the work surface and start kneading. Sometimes the dough will appear too dry to work, sometimes too wet and claggy. Simply add a little more water for the former, and sprinkle with a little more flour for the latter, the dough should not feel sticky. After you have started working the dough vigorously with both hands, you will, from time to time, probably need to shake a little more flour on to the work surface. The dough will elongate into a sausage each time you work it, which you need to furl back into a ball shape again before repeating the process.

After 10 minutes, place the ball back in the bowl and cover the top with a clean linen tea towel, which you have wetted under the hot tap and wrung out. Leave at the side of the stove for about an hour, or until it has swollen to about twice its original volume and appears light and spongy. Turn the oven to

230°C/450°F/Gas 8 to warm up. Brush the insides of your bread tins with olive oil. Turn the dough out on to the work surface and divide it into three pieces with a sharp knife. Knock the air out of each loaf for three or four minutes, without kneading it, and place each loaf in its tin.

Re-cover with a hot, damp cloth, and leave in the warmth close by or on top of the oven for 20–25 minutes. Brush the top of each loaf with a little milk, and sprinkle over a handful of seeds. Put two loaves together on a higher shelf and one on a lower. Set the timer for 35 minutes, but it could take 40. You want a distinctive hollow sound when you tap the base of the bread while turning it out on to a rack with a palate knife. Allow it to cool for at least 40 minutes; bread is steamy, doughy and indigestible if you eat it too soon. These principles apply to all the other types of loaves I listed, and to rolls, which naturally take less time to cook. When you are using a plain flour and wish to add seeds to the actual bread mix, throwing in a handful of all three types of seeds – sunflower, sesame and poppy – seems to work beautifully.

WHITE LOAF

Here is a sensationally good white loaf made with Shipton Mill's strong white flour, a handful of their newly toasted, deliciously oily wheatgerm and an overnight or overday rise to maximize the fermentation. I now bake bread on a terracotta stone. It should be a thick one according to John, but my pizza stone does two loaves beautifully. It radiates the heat evenly and there are no tin sides to give you a less crusty crust. Heat transfer is critical during baking and stones radiate heat in a totally different way to a metal tin. I also throw in a splash of water or squirt it into the oven with my iron spray – the steam helps to caramelize the surface of the loaf. I think it works best after the loaf has been in the oven for 10 minutes, but see what you think.

Makes 2 loaves

1kg/2¼lb Shipton Mill traditional organic strong white flour

3 tsp fine sea salt

45g/1½oz fresh yeast (you can buy it at the bread counter of your supermarket if they have an instore bakery)

570ml/1 pint warm water at 30°C in summer, 40°C in winter. To guess the temperature, it needs to be hand-hot, not boiling.

Allow approximately 14½ hours from the time you start the dough to cooking your bread. Dissolve a piece of yeast the size of a pea in 120ml/4fl oz of warm water in a jug. I stir the yeast in with a tiny whisk. Leave it for 10 minutes, then add it to 200g/7oz of the flour to which you have added half a teaspoonful of fine sea salt. Mix the dough a little with your fingers until it just coheres, then cover it with a tea towel soaked in cold water and wrung out – this prevents a skin forming. Leave it for 12 hours at room temperature in the kitchen. I have left bread dough a couple of hours longer when convenient and it has not come to any harm.

When the 12 hours are up, dissolve the remaining yeast in 120ml/4fl oz of warm water, whisking it as before. Leave it for 10–15 minutes in the warmth of the kitchen. It won't froth up as it does with a quick-rise bread when you add the sugar to the yeast and water at this stage.

Mix the rest of the bag of flour with the remaining salt and throw in a handful of wheatgerm. Add the starter dough, which will be spongy, to the mixture, then the yeasty liquid followed by the remaining 340ml/12fl oz of warm water. Work it in the bowl with your fingers until it coheres, then remove it to the work surface and knead energetically for 8–10 minutes.

Put the dough back in the large bowl, cover with the damp cloth again, and leave it for an hour to rise; it will double in volume. Put the dough back on the work surface, seize it, and bash the air out of it, then leave it uncovered for 15 minutes.

Preheat the oven to 220°C/425°F/Gas 7 and put the baking stone on the middle shelf to heat up. Divide the dough into two pieces with a knife and bash out the air again. Form each piece into a ball and cover with a damp cloth for 50 minutes. It will double in size again. Snip a little decorative hole or two in the middle of the top, scatter a tiny bit of flour over and, with a flat spatula,

plop the loaves on to the hot stone. After 10 minutes, spray or throw a little water into the oven until the steam hisses. The loaves will need 35–40 minutes. Check that the bottoms sound hollow before leaving the loaves to cool for an hour on a wire rack.

BROWN SODA BREAD

This is the bread to make if you don't, won't make bread. None of that watching yeast bubble, dough rise and double, and keeping things warm under cover of damp cloths. Soda bread is for beginners — short-of-time, easy-to-make delicious bread, which friends of mine in Ireland bake daily and as quickly as it takes to read this bit of cajolery. I find that the coarse wholemeal Ballybrado flour in Ireland is the best thing for the job, so try and use the coarsest stoneground flour you can find and add some toasted wheatgerm to it if you have a mind to. Shipton Mill's is the best I know. Great with banana jam.

Makes a 450g/1lb loaf

170g/6oz organic
  stoneground wholewheat
  flour
285g/10oz organic
  wholewheat flour
1 heaped tsp bicarbonate
  of soda
1 tsp salt
1 tsp molasses sugar
30g/1oz butter
480–570ml/16–20fl oz
  buttermilk

Preheat the oven to 230°C/450°F/Gas 8. Mix all the dry ingredients together with your hands, lightly rubbing in the butter. Make a well in the centre and add about 450ml/16fl oz of the buttermilk. Working from the centre with a knife, gather the mixture to make a soft, wet dough. You may have to add more buttermilk to make the mixture 'sticky wet'.

Grease a 450g/1lb round or oblong loaf tin, spoon in the dough and bake for 30 minutes. Cover the top with greaseproof paper and bake for a further 10–15 minutes. Turn out on to a wire rack and cover with a tea towel. Leave to cool slightly before attempting to slice the bread.

BANANA JAM

400g/13oz bananas, peeled
  weight
4 tsp fresh lemon juice
4 tsp pure pineapple juice
200g/7oz unrefined caster
  sugar
3 tsp fruit pectin

Mash the bananas roughly and place in a large saucepan with the rest of the ingredients. Place over a medium heat and whisk until the mixture boils. Remove from the heat and place in a large jar. Allow to cool to room temperature before chilling.

GOOSEBERRY OR RASPBERRY MUFFINS

Industrially baked, leaden, liberal-on-the-baking-powder muffins give a great cake a bad name. These are the best – light, delicately spiced with a burst of berried fruit and a top-crunch. Something to be enjoyed for breakfast, tea or at any time of day.

Makes 7 muffins

Whatever fruit is in season,
  gooseberries, raspberries,
  blueberries, blackberries,
  7 or 8 berries per muffin
200g/7oz self-raising flour
1 tsp baking powder
110g/4oz caster sugar
1 tsp ground cinnamon
75g/2½oz melted unsalted
  butter
1 egg
90ml/3fl oz milk
90ml/3fl oz plain yoghurt
1 tsp vanilla extract

Crumble topping
55g/2oz flour
55g/2oz butter
55g/2oz unrefined granulated
  sugar

Preheat the oven to 170°C/325°F/Gas 3. Sieve the flour, baking powder, sugar and cinnamon together into a bowl. Mix the butter, egg, milk, yoghurt and vanilla extract in a separate bowl, then add to the dry ingredients. Mix in whatever berries you have available.

Divide the mixture into individual greased muffin tins. Blitz the topping ingredients together in a food processor and sprinkle a teaspoon or so over the top of each muffin. Bake for 35–40 minutes. Transfer to a wire rack and leave to cool, or eat while still warm.

PLUM AND RHUBARB COMPOTE

Look for tender pink stems of rhubarb and discard anything green — it will taste acidic. This is great for breakfast with Greek yoghurt and granola, or for supper with cream.

Heat the oven to 150°C/300°F/Gas 2. Cut the rhubarb into batons rather than chunks, and put into a dish with the plums. Sprinkle on the sugar, then cover with greaseproof paper and a lid. Water is not necessary — the fruit will create its own juice.

Bake low down in the oven and test after 20 minutes. It may need longer, but the rhubarb should retain its shape and texture. Eat it chilled.

Serves 4

450g/1lb rhubarb
8 deep red, rather than
   golden, plums
half muscovado, half vanilla
   caster sugar to taste
   (3–4 tbsp)

GRANOLA

Sally Clarke's recipe for granola is such a state secret that she vows she'd give her grandmother away first, so either buy it from her Kensington shop (ring 020 7229 2190 for stockists), or make this fabulous version from one of my favourite chefs, Yotam at Ottolenghi in Notting Hill (020 7727 1121).

Makes one large jar

30g/1oz pure maple syrup
2 dsrtsp sunflower oil
1 tbsp warm water
45g/1½oz light muscovado
½ tsp salt
110g/4oz organic jumbo oats
55g/2oz whole almonds
30g/1oz brazil nuts, broken up

Whisk together the maple syrup, oil and water with the muscovado sugar and salt. Add the oats and nuts and mix everything together well.

Spread the mixture on a baking tray lined with greaseproof paper, making sure it is not piled more than 1.5cm/½in high. Bake at 140°C/275°F/Gas 1 for about an hour, stirring once half way through. Remove the granola from the oven and let it cool down before storing in a sealed container.

PAIN PERDU
OR POOR KNIGHTS OF WINDSOR WITH JAM SAUCE

This lovely medieval dish, eaten in both England and France, was originally made with bread baked from the finest flour, which was dipped in beaten egg before frying, spicing and sugaring. Today, the Americans call it French toast, but the original names have the romantic edge.

Serves 4–6

6 slices of day-old good bread
4 tbsp single cream
3 eggs, preferably organic
1 tbsp sherry or Madeira
unsalted butter
caster sugar
cinnamon

Jam sauce
1 x 225g/8oz jar raspberry jam
1–2 tbsp water
spritz of lemon juice
1 tbsp Cognac (optional)

Remove or leave the crusts on the bread, according to your preference, then cut each slice diagonally into two triangles. Whisk the cream, eggs and sherry thoroughly in a bowl, then soak each side of the bread in the mixture.

Melt the butter in a frying pan, and slip in the slices of egged bread before the butter browns. Fry them on both sides until they are browned and crisp. Put them into a warmed serving dish and sprinkle with a little sugar and cinnamon. Serve with jam sauce.

JAM SAUCE

Slowly melt the jam in a small pan with a tablespoon of water and the lemon juice. Judge whether it needs slackening a little with more water. Add the alcohol if you are using it and, when hot, put the sauce in a jug to pour over the pain perdu. Strawberry, cherry, blackberry, blackcurrant or apricot jams work equally well.

JUICES

These are something to experiment with if you have a Maserati machine like I do, a Waring juicer. Too sharp with too sharp, mild with sharp are obviously things to avoid. Pears get drowned out by citrus, berries, sharp apples or exotic fruit. Peaches lose it to mangoes, but mango, banana and apple are great together. Pulpy fruit such as mango and banana need juicy apples to help thin them down.

Peaches with a few raspberries and some apples thrown in are great, or just grunge up the peaches to drink solo or as a Bellini, the greatest cocktail invention ever, with Prosecco. Pineapple froths and thins down to an exotically sharp and lovely drink to stick in a tall jug and serve with crushed ice.

3

Saturday lunch

Soups, salads, tarts, bread, cheese, fruit — unfussy,
uncluttered food — these are the things that make the best
Saturday lunches. You want one or two perfect flavours
and textures — good bread, a slice of creamy-fatted,
garnet-hued pata negra ham or prosciutto, a good,
oozingly ripe slice of unpasteurized Montgomery cheddar
with a fig or a scoop of tomato chilli jam.

WATERCRESS, PEAR AND ROQUEFORT SALAD
WITH TOASTED SESAME SEEDS

Watercress is best eaten raw, and here the peppery leaves are contrasted with creamy, salty cheese, sweet pear, mellow vinegar and fruity olive oil. Simple perfection if you use only the best ingredients.

Serves 2

a bunch of organic watercress
2 ripe pears, peeled and
  rubbed with a little lemon
  juice to keep them from
  discolouring
110g/4oz best Roquefort (I
  favour Papillon or Troupeau)
a fruity olive oil, such as
  Ravida from Sicily
a well-aged balsamic vinegar
  (ideally 20 years or more)
a handful of sesame seeds
sea salt and black pepper

Wash and dry the watercress and heap it on to each plate. Add the peeled, cored and quartered pears and creamy lumps of cheese.

Make a dressing with the olive oil and balsamic vinegar (two parts oil to one part balsamic), adding sea salt and a scrunch of black pepper. Toast a handful of sesame seeds in a hot oven until they turn golden and nutty smelling. Five minutes should do it, but keep checking as they are the easiest of things to burn. Pour a libation of the dressing over each portion of the salad, sprinkle with sesame seeds and eat.

SMOKE-ROASTED SALMON, WATERCRESS
AND HORSERADISH SANDWICH

I ate my first smoke-roasted salmon sandwich with watercress and horseradish on Hobbs House peerless bread at The Fine Cheese Company in Bath. Now when I suffer withdrawal, I make my own.

Serves 1

1 portion smoke-roasted
  salmon
grated horseradish
crème fraîche
a little lemon juice (optional)
two thick slices of good
  crusted bread
a bunch of organic watercress

Stir a teaspoon of horseradish into a heaped dessertspoon of crème fraîche. Taste and adjust according to how hot you like it. Add a drop of lemon juice and spread on each slice of bread.

Put a hefty clump of watercress, then chunks of smoke-roasted salmon on one slice, press the other slice on top and eat immediately.

POTATO AND PORCINI FOCACCIA

I add a little honey to help speed the dried yeast. If you're using fresh yeast, there is no need to add the honey.

Makes 2 loaves

340ml/12fl oz warm sparkling bottled water (the increased bi-soda content gives a lighter, crisper loaf)
1 tsp easy-blend yeast
1 tsp runny honey
450g/1lb strong white flour
1 tsp malt extract (you can buy it at health-food shops)
2 tsp fine sea salt
10 tbsp extra-virgin olive oil

Topping

1 large potato, unpeeled, washed and finely sliced on a mandoline if possible
1 small onion, finely sliced
2 fresh porcini, or a handful of sliced dried mushrooms
2 tbsp extra-virgin olive oil
2 tsp Maldon sea salt

In a small bowl, mix together 200ml/7fl oz water, the yeast and the honey. Whisk together until the yeast has dissolved, then whisk in 140g/5oz flour. Cover the bowl with clingfilm and leave in a warm place for two hours, giving the mixture a stir after the first hour. By this time it should be bubbling and have risen to double its original height. This is called the 'sponge' and it will be the ferment that aerates the final dough.

Scrape the sponge into another larger bowl, then add the remaining water and the malt extract and whisk together until the sponge has more or less combined with the water. Add the remaining flour and the salt and squidge the mixture together with your hand (try to do this with one hand to keep the other clean and dry). The mixture will be very soft, slightly lumpy and very sticky. This is good.

Scrape the dough down from around the sides of the bowl, then give your hands a good wash to remove any excess dough. Remove the dough from the bowl, tip a tablespoon of the olive oil on to your hands and rub the oil all over the surface of the dough.

Place the oiled dough on the worktop and knead five times (about 10 seconds). Cover with clingfilm and leave for 10 minutes. Rub another tablespoon of oil over the surface and knead 12 times (about 20 seconds). Cover and leave to prove for 30 minutes.

Knead a further 12 times, then cover and leave for 30 minutes. Heat the oven to 230°C/450°F/Gas 8. Take two 30 x 40cm/12 x 16in trays and rub the insides liberally with olive oil. In a bowl, mix together the thinly sliced potatoes, onions and mushrooms with two tablespoons of olive oil and a pinch of salt. Stir until the potato slices are well coated with the oil.

Divide the dough in two and knead each piece into a ball. Place each ball on a tray and lightly flatten with a rolling pin. Don't worry if the dough springs back. Cover with clingfilm and leave in a warm place for 20–30 minutes.

Pick up the corners of the dough and stretch them out until they reach the corners of the tray. Tip the potato mixture evenly on top of each sheet of dough. Cover with clingfilm and leave a further 15 minutes. Remove the clingfilm, dimple the surface of the dough with your fingers, add a little extra salt if you wish and bake for 30–45 minutes, until the surface is golden and the potatoes tender. Remove from the oven and slide on to a cooling rack.

AUBERGINE, FETA AND MINT SALAD

Aubergine slices soak up oil like nobody's business. Cooking them in the oven like this makes sure they are tender but not drenched and sodden with oil.

Preheat the oven to 200°C/400°F/Gas 6. Line a baking tray with baking parchment. Cut the aubergines into thick rounds, brush both sides with olive oil and lay on the baking tray.

Cook for 15 minutes until soft and browned – check with a skewer to make sure they are done. Leave to cool slightly. While still warm, layer the slices in a serving dish with crumbled feta and torn leaves of mint. Season each layer with black pepper. Drizzle over a little oil but don't overdo it – the slices will be oily already. Spritz with lemon juice.

Serves 4 as an appetizer

2 medium aubergines
extra-virgin olive oil
110g/4oz feta cheese
a few sprigs of mint
lemon juice
black pepper

ASPARAGUS, FENNEL AND RED PEPPER SALAD

Loath as I am to eat asparagus in any form that isn't as near as damn it au naturel, this salad, which my friend George Morley suggested we make one greedy weekend, quite converted me; it makes a brilliant starter. The peppers don't overwhelm, so the asparagus is allowed to play the starring role.

Serves 6

2 organic red peppers
2 large bundles of asparagus,
   450g/1lb each
2 bulbs fennel
olive oil, lemon juice, salt and
   pepper, and a sprinkling of
   chervil if you have it to hand

Grill the peppers on all sides and put them in a bowl under clingfilm so the skins begin to steam off. Skin, de-seed and cut them into thin strips. Cut the asparagus into 5cm/2in chunks, and steam the stalks on their own for a couple of minutes. Add the tips, and steam until cooked, about another three minutes.

Remove the outer layer of the fennel bulbs down to the firm heart, and slice them as thinly as you can, with a mandolin if you have one. Put all the vegetables into a bowl, then pour in your oil and lemon dressing, and mix together gently by hand. Serve with a good crusted bread like Boule de Meule.

MOROCCAN CARROT SALAD
WITH GARLIC AND CORIANDER

This is one of the many wonderful dishes Sami cooks at Ottolenghi in London's Notting Hill, my favourite traiteur / Viennoiserie / café.

Serves 4

500g/1lb 2oz carrots, peeled
   and cut into sticks
4 cloves of garlic, peeled
4 tbsp olive oil
2 tbsp cider vinegar
1 tsp cumin, roasted in a pan
   then ground
1 tsp paprika
sea salt and black pepper
2 tbsp chopped fresh
   coriander

Cover the carrots in a saucepan with boiling, salted water, adding the garlic, and cook until tender but not soft. Drain, crush the garlic cloves and add them to the carrots with the remaining ingredients, leaving aside half the coriander.

Transfer to a serving dish while hot and sprinkle over the rest of the coriander. I served this at room temperature, but it can be served hot or cold.

TOMATOES BAKED WITH OLIVES, MUSTARD AND GRUYÈRE

An unshowy and versatile dish — you can eat it in its own right as a starter or light lunch, or it can equally well partner a grilled chicken or a pork chop as a more substantial main course. If you look snobbishly down on the much maligned stuffed tomato, think again. I know you will reconsider if you try this dish. You can prepare the tomatoes several hours in advance before cooking.

Serves 4

8 ripe medium-sized organic
    tomatoes
16 best black olives
a sprig of fresh thyme
1 tbsp black olive paste, the
    best are Seggiano and
    Carluccio
1 tbsp Dijon mustard
a handful of breadcrumbs
    made with day-old bread,
    white or wholemeal
110g/4oz Gruyère cheese,
    grated
olive oil
sea salt and pepper

Preheat oven to 220°C/425°F/Gas 7. Cut the tomatoes in half horizontally and scoop out the seeds and core with a teaspoon. Place them cut side up on a baking tray, season and plop a pitted olive inside each half.

Rub a few thyme leaves from their sprig with your fingers into the olive paste, then stir in the mustard and brush it over the tomatoes. Mix the breadcrumbs with half the grated Gruyère and stuff the tomatoes. Put the rest of the grated cheese on top and pour a slug of olive oil over each tomato half.

You are now ready to bake, but you can leave these prepared tomatoes for a few hours before cooking them if it suits you. Bake for 20 minutes and serve warm, with a good hunk of bread or a roll if you feel like it.

TORTILLA ESPANOLA

Said to have been invented by a peasant for a hungry king, this dish has been cooked in Spain for at least 400 years. Every tapas bar seems to serve tortilla, with glasses of chilled fino or manzanilla, and although the classic rendering is made with potato, you may substitute onion, prawns, peppers, spinach, chard or what you will. I think tortillas make the perfect mouthful to accompany drinks, so absorbent are they, like blotting paper, arresting initial hunger pangs and any light-headedness concomitantly. Tortilla can be served hot, warm or cold.

Serves 4

450g/1lb potatoes, peeled
    and cut into small dice
6 large organic eggs
110ml/4fl oz best olive oil
sea salt and freshly ground
    pepper

Do not use a voluminous frying pan, you are making a cake of eggs, not a flat omelette. Heat the olive oil, and when it is hot, throw in the potatoes and coat them all over in the oil. Lower the heat and turn them gently every so often until they are cooked through. Remove the potatoes with a slotted spoon and drain them on kitchen paper in a bowl.

Heat the olive oil in the pan again, with a bit extra if you need it. Meanwhile, beat the eggs with the pepper and pour them over the potatoes, then pour the mixture into the hot oil in the pan and cook at a high heat for a minute before turning the temperature down. Add salt and cook until there is no sign of liquid egg at the top of the mixture. Cover with a plate and flip the tortilla over on to it, add a splosh more olive oil to the pan, then slide the tortilla back into the pan and cook for a further couple of minutes.

Serve hot or warm with a tomato sauce, on its own or with some Navarrico piquillo peppers, roasted over beech wood and imported by Brindisa. Or eat it cold and cut into wedges with a tomato salad. Once cooked, a tortilla will keep for a couple of days, and reheats well in a tomato sauce.

BROAD BEANS
WITH PRESERVED LEMON, CORIANDER AND SPANISH PAPRIKA

Another dish from Ottolenghi in Notting Hill. It is best made with the first little pods of broad beans, but I'm not purist about this one – frozen beans will do. After all, they're getting revved up with spices and preserved lemons. This dish makes a lovely salad, mezze or starter or a good accompaniment to lamb or chicken with couscous.

Serves 4

500g/1lb 2oz small broad beans (frozen are fine but thaw them first)
1 large onion, thinly sliced
1 tbsp Spanish paprika
1 tsp cumin, roasted in a pan then ground
4 tbsp extra virgin olive oil
6 tbsp water
sea salt and black pepper
1 medium bunch of coriander, coarsely chopped
half a preserved lemon, thinly sliced
juice of a lemon

Put the broad beans, onion, paprika, cumin, olive oil and water in a large saucepan. Season, cover and bring to the boil. Turn down the heat and simmer until the beans are just cooked (about 10 minutes). You may need to add a little more water during the cooking.

Add the chopped coriander, preserved lemon and lemon juice, then adjust the seasoning. Serve hot or warm.

BAZARGAN OR CRACKED WHEAT AND NUT SALAD

This inspirational Syrian dish is from Claudia Roden's seminal 'The Book of Jewish Food'. The sourness of the pomegranate molasses or tamarind gives the grain a delicious sharp sweet flavour and colours the bulgur, which should be of the coarse kind.

Roden advises making it four hours before serving so that the wheat absorbs the dressing properly. I made mine with pomegranate molasses, and only four scant tablespoons of tomato paste.

Serves 6–8

340g/12oz bulgur (cracked wheat)
6–8 tbsp extra virgin olive oil
3 tbsp pomegranate molasses or 2 tbsp tamarind paste dissolved in 4 tbsp boiling water
juice of a lemon
4 tbsp tomato paste
1 tsp ground cumin
1 tsp ground coriander
½ tsp ground allspice
½ tsp ground cayenne or chilli pepper, or to taste
140g/5oz walnuts, very coarsely chopped
100g/3½oz hazelnuts, very coarsely chopped
55g/2oz pine nuts, lightly toasted
a large bunch flat-leaf parsley, finely chopped

Put the cracked wheat into a large bowl and cover with plenty of cold, slightly salted water. Leave to soak for an hour or until tender (the coarse bulgur takes much longer). Drain in a sieve and press out the excess water.

In a serving bowl, beat the olive oil with the pomegranate molasses or dissolved tamarind paste. Add the lemon juice, tomato paste, cumin, coriander, allspice and cayenne and beat well. Pour over the cracked wheat and mix thoroughly. Add the nuts and flat-leaf parsley, mix again and adjust the seasoning if necessary.

CRÊPES PARMENTIER
WITH SMOKED EEL, CRISPY BACON AND HORSERADISH

I remember a fantastic dish of eels stewed with crispy belly pork and garlic in the original Poons restaurant in Lisle Street in Soho. I think the affinity between eel and bacon is sublime. Here they are both smoked, so it's a head-on, full-strength flavour, with the creamiest of little starchy potato pancakes and a hit of horseradish. You can prepare the batter a few hours before you want it, and the horseradish, leaving your guests with the assembly job.

Serves 6 as a starter

2 fillets of smoked eel
8 rashers organic oak-smoked
  streaky bacon

Crêpes Parmentier
450g/1lb floury organic
  potatoes, peeled and
  cooked
60ml/2fl oz milk
2 heaped tbsp potato or
  ordinary flour
3 eggs and 4 whites
2 tbsp double cream
salt and pepper
butter

Horseradish cream
small carton of double or
  soured cream
fresh horseradish root, grated
lemon
salt

First make the crêpes. Put the hot potatoes through the coarse disc of the mouli, or mash by hand. Put them into a bowl with the milk, flour, eggs, whites, cream and seasoning, and whisk together. Heat a tiny bit of clarified, unsalted butter in your pancake pan, and add tablespoons of the mixture, several if your pan is big enough, flipping the pancakes over with a palette knife when they begin to bubble and brown around the edge; a couple of minutes.

Keep warm on a plate in a warm oven while you make the rest. Allow a rasher of streaky bacon per person and throw in a couple extra, and fry in their own fat until curled and crispened.

For the horseradish cream, I use either double cream or soured cream. If you can't get hold of fresh horseradish root, the only commercial brands I know that don't turn it into a noxious paste are the English Provender Company's Hot Horseradish, stocked by good supermarkets, and Source Foods Organic Horseradish Relish. Ring 01495 371698 for stockists.

Depending on whether you want a runny or a stiffer result, do or do not whip the cream. Then stir in the horseradish a teaspoon at a time, tasting as you go. There is no going back! A spritz of lemon and a sprinkle of salt, and you have it.

Skin and fillet your eel by literally unpeeling it in one swift, satisfying move. Then chop your two fillets into 5cm/2in chunks, and put one on each pancake, followed by the bacon and a dollop of horseradish cream.

KIRKHAM'S LANCASHIRE CHEESE AND APPLE TART

The perfect combination of deliciously lactic, crumbly Lancashire cheese with sweet, crisp eating apples makes a highly unusual tart: it can be served as successfully as a main course as it can as a pudding.

Caerphilly would do if you can't find the superb, traditionally made Lancashire. You want a crumbly lactic cheese with a fruity, acid flavour, not a melting, salty cheese.

Serves 6

55g/2oz unsalted butter
5 large Granny Smith apples,
  peeled, cored and sliced
2 onions, thinly sliced
225g/8oz Kirkham's
  Lancashire cheese, coarsely
  grated
1 tsp fresh thyme leaves
salt and black pepper
1 small egg, beaten

Shortcrust pastry
225g/8oz flour
110g/4oz unsalted butter
1 tsp fresh thyme leaves

Make the shortcrust pastry, adding a teaspoon of fresh thyme leaves to the mixture. Chill, then divide into two balls, one slightly larger than the other, and roll out thinly. Preheat the oven to 180°C/350°F/Gas 4.

Melt the butter in a heavy-bottomed frying pan, then add the apples and onions and cook gently until softened, 15–20 minutes. Remove from the heat and stir in the cheese, thyme and seasoning, then leave to cool.

Fit the larger layer of pastry into a 23–25cm/9–10 in loose-bottomed tart tin or shallow pie plate, then heap on the filling. Cover with the top layer of pastry, seal and crimp the edges, and cut a cross in the middle for the steam to escape through. Brush the top with beaten egg and cook for 35–40 minutes. Serve warm.

PAN BAGNAT

*This is really a Niçoise salad sealed inside a loaf, the name 'pan bagnat'
literally meaning wet bread. I have always been pretty liberal minded with my
interpretation of the ingredients, including the type of bread – baguette,
ciabatta or rolls all being good vehicles. If you have time to weight the pan
bagnat wrapped in foil on a plate overnight for all the juices and oil to
mingle, it is best of all. Otherwise, the types of olives and beans, broad or
French, the addition and subtraction of artichokes, eggs, fish, onions,
cucumber, and basil or other herbs, is all your own. Use your imagination.*

Serves 6–8

6 large good-flavoured
  organic tomatoes, skinned
1 red pepper or a jar of
  roasted peppers
1 shallot or small onion,
  peeled
225g/8oz shelled broad beans
3 softly hard-boiled eggs
4 artichoke hearts, Seggiano's
  roasted in oil are sublime
6 salted anchovies,
  desalinated, despined and
  split in half
a small jar of best bonita tuna
  from Brindisa, or 'ventresca',
  belly of tuna
a clove of garlic
1 tbsp of red wine vinegar
olive oil
a handful of pitted olives,
  Niçoise if possible
a handful of torn basil leaves
baguette, ciabatta or rolls

Cut the tomatoes into eighths, cut the pepper into strips and slice the onion
and artichokes. Blanch the broad beans for a minute and slip off the skins if you
can be bothered. Mix the vegetables together. Peel the eggs and slice them.
Drain the tuna.

Slice the bread or rolls horizontally and scoop out some of the bread from
both halves. Rub both with a cut clove of garlic, then sprinkle over the vinegar
and oil to dress the loaf. Pile a layer of vegetables on to the bottom half, then
add the egg, tuna and olives. Scatter basil leaves on top and add diagonal strips
of anchovy. Put the top deck of bread over the heaped salad and wrap in foil.
Place on a plate, weigh down and leave overnight if possible. Cut the pan
bagnat into slices to serve.

ROASTED PUMPKIN AND COCONUT SOUP
WITH THAI SPICES

This soup is best with butternut or red onion squash, even sweet potato, rather than English pumpkin, which has no flavour.

Serves 4

1 butternut or red onion
  squash (about 750g/
  1lb 10oz)
olive oil
75g/2½oz of creamed
  coconut
1 onion
1 stalk lemongrass
1 bird's-eye chilli
1 thumb of galangal, grated
  (or use root ginger and a
  squeeze of lime)

Cut the squash into chunks and remove the seeds. Brush the chunks with oil and roast at 200°C/400°F/Gas 6 for 20–25 minutes. Add 200ml/7 fl oz of hot water to the coconut and mix well.

Finely chop the onion and sauté in olive oil. Add a split stalk of lemongrass, the chilli, deseeded and chopped, and the grated galangal or root ginger. When the squash is cool enough to handle, remove the peel and add the flesh to the onion and spices in the pan.

Add more hot water to the coconut mixture to bring it up to 900ml/32fl oz. Pour on to the vegetables and spices and simmer gently for 15 minutes. Remove the lemongrass and whizz the soup in a liquidizer until smooth. Serve with a swirl of crème fraîche and some chopped coriander.

EASY ROAST CHERRY TOMATO SOUP

A perfect late-summer lunch, deeply flavoured, yet made without butter, oil or cream, and strong tasting enough to survive in a flask at sea.

Serves 4–5

1kg/2¼lb organic cherry
  tomatoes
3 cloves of garlic in their skins
1.2 litres/2 pints intense jellied
  chicken stock; mine was
  made by poaching 2 fowl
  and then making a further
  stock of the carcasses and
  poaching liquor with
  vegetables
1 heaped tsp muscovado
  sugar
salt and pepper

Roast the tomatoes in a roasting tin with the garlic for about an hour in a medium oven. The skins will have split, and the juices run.

Allow the tomatoes to cool until you can handle them, then skin them and the garlic, and put in the blender with two or three ladles of the hot stock. Whizz, then sieve, including the skins from which you can press the flavour.

Return to the pan with the rest of the stock, add the sugar and seasoning to taste, and serve. I resist the usual urge for basil, butter, cream or parsley. This soup is intensely enough flavoured as it is, and utterly simple to make.

CHEESE AND THYME SCONES

I serve these with the Roast Cherry Tomato Soup above. They form a delicious crusty lattice of russet-coloured baked cheese on top, and are suitably filling and tasty to stand up to the broth. Start making them half an hour before the soup is ready.

Makes 12 scones

50g/1½oz butter
225g/8oz organic strong
  white flour
a pinch of sea salt
1 tbsp baking powder
110g/4oz good strong
  cheddar
1 tsp English mustard powder
2 tsp fresh thyme leaves
a pinch of cayenne pepper
150ml/5fl oz of milk

Preheat the oven to 200°C/400°F/Gas 6.

Rub the butter into the sifted flour, salt and baking powder in a bowl. Add two-thirds of the coarsely grated cheese and the mustard, thyme and cayenne, and then gradually cut the milk in with a knife; you might not need it all but you want a soft dough. Roll it out to 1.5cm/¾in thickness, then cut with an upturned glass or pastry cutter.

Put the scones on a buttered baking tray, sprinkle with the remaining cheese, and bake for 12–15 minutes. Set on a wire rack for five minutes, then eat hot with lashings of good country butter.

CHICKEN SOUP

This is the most comforting dish in the world and a dish you can play around with according to the season. Your base stock has to be good. Some like chicken soup thick, some like it thin; some like their vegetables puréed, some diced. My children like it thick and gluey, with doll's-size diced vegetables.

Serves 8

Stock

1 large or 2 small chicken
  carcasses from a cooked
  bird, with 110–170g/4–6oz
  of dark and light meat
  stripped off to add at the
  end of cooking
2 or 3 onions, halved, in their
  skins
2 or 3 stalks celery, broken in
  two, with the leaves
3 or 4 carrots, chopped in
  chunks
2 or 3 leeks, cleaned, the
  green and the white
a small bunch of parsley
6–8 peppercorns

Soup

2 litres/3½ pints chicken stock
1 small potato
1 parsnip and 1 carrot, peeled
  and chopped into tiny dice
2 celery stalks with their
  leaves, strung with a potato
  peeler, then finely chopped
a bulb of fennel, outer leaves
  removed, finely diced
two large handfuls of frozen
  or fresh petits pois
110–170g/4–6oz dark and
  light chicken meat, cut small
  along the grain of the flesh
2 tbsp cornflour
150ml/5fl oz double cream
sea salt and black pepper
parsley

Break the carcasses into two or three bits with your fingers and put them with the leftover bones and skin in a huge, heavy-bottomed pot. Heat gently, until the bones begin to brown and the skin starts to release its fat, then add the vegetables, parsley, peppercorns and enough water to cover. Bring to the boil slowly, then skim. Turn down to a simmer, put the lid on and bubble for a couple of hours.

Strain the liquid into a large bowl, pressing down on the vegetables. Throw all the contents of the strainer away. Allow the liquid to cool and refrigerate, if necessary, before using. Then remove the stock from the fridge and scoop off the solidified fat from the surface.

To make the soup, bring the stock to boiling point, then throw in the potato. After five minutes of gentle simmering, throw in the parsnip and carrot and, five minutes later, the celery and fennel. Cook until nearly softened before adding the peas for five minutes. Add the pieces of chicken now. Remove a couple of ladles of the hot stock from the pan to a bowl in which you've put the cornflour and stir with a small whisk until free of lumps.

Return to the pan, add the cream, season and bring to boiling point. Serve with a scattering of parsley.

COS LETTUCE
WITH CASHEL BLUE AND A CREAM DRESSING

Cashel Blue is a richly creamy blue Irish cheese, fudgy textured with no hint of bitterness. It is delicious crumbled into this salad of cos hearts.

Stir the first four ingredients together in a bowl with the egg yolk, then stir in the cream. Thin with a bit of milk or water if it has thickened too much.

Pour cold over the washed lettuce, then scatter over the chopped egg white, chives and coarsely crumbled Cashel Blue.

Serves 6

1 tsp French mustard
1 tsp sugar
2 tsp tarragon vinegar
a scrap of crushed garlic
1 hard-boiled egg, white and
   yolk separated
200–250ml/7–8½fl oz double
   cream
2 dsrtsp chives, chopped
110–170g/4–6oz Cashel Blue
2 heads of cos lettuce, outer
   leaves removed; keep them
   for soup

TOMATO CHILLI JAM
WITH GOAT'S CHEESE AND BRUSCHETTA

Quite simply, your kitchen should never be without this jam; it keeps in the fridge for weeks if it is allowed the chance to do so. Great with a Montgomery Cheddar sandwich, in a toasted sandwich, or piled on to bruschetta over some slices of Ragstone or Golden Cross goat's cheese.

Makes 2 large jars

750g/1lb 10 oz very ripe organic tomatoes
4 red chillies, with their seeds
6 fat cloves of garlic, peeled
3 thumbs of fresh ginger, peeled and roughly chopped
40 ml/1½fl oz Thai fish sauce, (nam pla)
450g/1lb unrefined golden caster sugar
150ml/5fl oz red wine vinegar

Bruschetta
good bread
goat's cheese, such as Ragstone or Golden Cross

Blend half the tomatoes, the chillies, garlic, ginger and fish sauce to a fine purée in a blender. You need the chilli seeds for the heat, which is not intense, and the tomato seeds for the pectin that will make the jam set.

Put the purée, sugar and vinegar into a deep pan and bring slowly to the boil slowly, stirring all the time. When it reaches the boil, turn down to a gentle simmer and add the remaining tomatoes cut into tiny dice, about 5mm/¼in, skin and all. Skim off the foam and cook gently for about an hour and a quarter to an hour and a half, stirring every so often to release the solids that settle on the bottom and prevent them from burning. Be sure to scrape the sides of the pot too, so the entire mass cooks evenly.

When the jam is done, pour it into warmed glass jars. Allow it to cool to room temperature before storing in the fridge or a cold larder for later use.

BRUSCHETTA
To make bruschetta, cut some thick slices of good bread, daub them with olive oil and crisp them on both sides in a hot oven. Serve with slices of warmed goat cheese, topped with tomato chilli jam.

4

Tea time

This, like Christmas, I can't help feeling is really for children. If we all took tea seriously every day, we'd be as wide as we are tall. But — occasional indulgence is a wonderful thing, and breaking the afternoon with a mouthwatering cake, cookie or biscuit is what the weekend is all about. Here are some old-fashioned and new-fangled treats, some of which make stunning puddings with a spoonful of crème fraîche or ice cream.

SOMERSET APPLE CAKE

This is as good served warm with crème fraîche for pudding as it is for tea as a simple cake. Soak the sultanas overnight in the cider.

Serves 6

225g/8oz unrefined caster
   sugar
170g/6oz unsalted butter
2 eggs
285g/10oz plain flour
1½ tsp baking powder
1 tsp cinnamon
zest of 1 lemon
2 large Bramley apples
170g/6oz sultanas
150ml/5fl oz good, dry cider

Preheat the oven to 170°C/325°F/Gas 3. Cream the sugar and butter thoroughly, add the eggs one at a time, beating as you go, then fold in the dry ingredients, the lemon zest and the thinly sliced apples.

Add the sultanas soaked in cider, along with any remaining cider. Bake in a greased, lined 20cm/8in springform tin for 45–50 minutes, or until a skewer comes out clean.

Cool in the tin, then remove the cake to a rack. Reheat it if you are serving it as a pudding with crème fraîche. Lace the crème fraîche with a little Calvados or Somerset cider brandy (optional).

ALMOND AND ORANGE FLORENTINES

As made at Ottolenghi, in Notting Hill, London, by Khalid Assyb.

Makes about 16

3 egg whites
140g/5oz unrefined icing
  sugar
400g/13oz flaked almonds
grated zest of 2 oranges

Preheat the oven to 150°C/300°F/Gas 2. Line a baking tray with silicone paper and brush lightly with vegetable oil. Mix all the ingredients by hand. Using a wet hand, make little mounds of the almond mix on the tray, spaced well apart. Dip a fork in water and flatten each biscuit until very thin.

Place in the oven and bake for about 12 minutes, until the florentines are golden brown. Cool before removing from the tray. They are delicious served with ice cream.

GINGER BISCUITS

Easy to make and perfect for a warming tea-time treat.

Makes about 30

110g/4oz butter
225g/8oz unrefined caster
  sugar
1 small egg
1 tbsp golden syrup
225g/8oz plain flour
2 tsp cinnamon
1 level tsp ground ginger
1 tsp bicarbonate of soda

Cream the butter with the sugar until light and fluffy. Add the egg, then the syrup and beat together well.

Mix the dry ingredients with the sieved flour and amalgamate well with the egg mixture. Knead into a lump, then break off walnut-sized pieces, roll them into balls and place on a greased baking tin. Bake for about 45 minutes in a slow oven, or until golden brown. Remove and leave to cool for a minute or two before transferring to a rack to cool further.

CHOCOLATE COOKIES

The resist factor is nil. So you don't like chocolate? OK, turn the page, but these are oozing, dark, delectable cookies rolled in icing sugar, their crust cracked like parched earth and sweetly crisped. I bludgeoned the recipe from the brilliant cooks at Ottolenghi in Notting Hill. Makes FAR MORE than you need, but the dough freezes brilliantly.

Makes dozens

340g/12oz good quality
 chocolate, 70% cocoa solids
340g/12oz butter, unsalted
3 eggs
450g/1lb light muscovado
 sugar
1 double espresso
500g/1lb 2 oz self-raising flour
1½ tsp baking powder
unrefined icing sugar to roll
 the cookies in

Gently melt the butter and chocolate together in a double boiler or in a bowl over, but not touching, hot water. Whisk the eggs and sugar in a food mixer for three minutes, then add the warm chocolate mix and the espresso. Sift the flour and baking powder and fold them into the mixture by hand. Wrap the dough in clingfilm and leave it to cool for a couple of hours before baking or put it in the fridge overnight.

When you are ready to bake the cookies, preheat the oven to 180°C/350°F/Gas 4. Take the dough and roll walnut-sized balls in your hand. Roll them in icing sugar. and put on silicone paper. Bake for 10–12 minutes and allow to cool on a rack.

CHOCOLATE BROWNIES

Quite the best, just don't overcook them. Brownies are meant to have a 'sad' centre, above which there is a thin, dry, slightly crunchy crust.

Makes 12–15 squares

200g/7oz best bitter
  chocolate
125g/4½oz unsalted butter,
  softened
225g/8oz vanilla caster sugar
2 eggs and 1 yolk
4 tbsp freshly made coffee
150g/5oz plain flour
1 tsp baking powder
a pinch of sea salt
a handful of broken walnuts,
  optional

Preheat the oven to 180°C/350°F/Gas 4. Place a piece of foil in the bottom and up the sides of a roasting tin or earthenware dish. Mine is about 30 x 23cm/12 x 9in.

Gently melt the chocolate in a double boiler or in a bowl over, but not touching, hot water. Cream the butter and sugar until really light and fluffy; I do this in the KitchenAid. With the mixer running, add the eggs, one at a time, then the yolk. Pour in the melted chocolate, then the coffee.

Remove the mixing bowl to a work surface and sift in the flour, baking powder and a pinch of salt. Fold them all in, also the walnuts. Pour the mixture into the tin, and bake for 20–25 minutes. A skewer inserted into the mixture should come out a bit sticky. The interior should be a sort of fudgy goo, not a sponge. Leave to cool before you cut the cake into squares and turn them out.

RICH CHOCOLATE CHIP AND HAZELNUT BROWNIES

Quite the best, too, so which ones are you going to do? I suggest you try them both. Size is your business, but this mixture fills a small roasting tin.

Makes 12–16 squares

285g/10oz unrefined caster
  sugar
4 eggs
225g/8oz unsalted butter
85g/3oz Green and Black's
  organic cocoa
85g/3oz plain flour
110g/4oz roasted hazelnuts
110g/4oz cooking chocolate
  chunks. The Chocolate
  Society do them in bags,
  70% cocoa solids

Preheat the oven to 180°C/350°F/Gas 4. Grease the roasting tin. Beat the sugar and eggs together really well, until they have thickened and the sugar has totally dissolved. Melt the butter and pour it into the sugar and egg mixture. Sieve the cocoa and flour together into the mixture, then stir them in.

Put the hazelnuts and chocolate chunks in a ziploc bag, and whack it as hard as you dare with a rolling pin, keeping things a little chunky. The nuts will be more pulverized than the chocolate. Fold into the mixture and scrape it into the baking tin. Bake for about 25 minutes. Test with a skewer. You don't want it to come out completely clean, but the mixture should not appear raw. Leave to cool before you cut the mixture into squares and remove them from the tin.

PARKIN

This wonderfully old-fashioned cake, rather like treacly-black, molasses-laden gingerbread, is best made a couple of days before you want to eat it, cut into squares.

Makes 12–16 squares

110g/4oz butter
85g/3oz light muscovado
  sugar
340g/12oz organic blackstrap
  molasses
225g/8oz plain or wholemeal
  flour
2 tsp baking powder
1 tsp ground root ginger
1 tsp mixed spice
salt
4 tbsp milk
flaked almonds (optional)

Preheat the oven to 180°C/350°F/Gas 4. Melt the butter, sugar and molasses together in a pan over a gentle heat. Remove from the heat and add to the remaining ingredients in a bowl, beating them together lightly until well amalgamated. Grease and line a roasting tin with greaseproof paper, pour in the mixture and bake for about 40 minutes, until just firm to the touch. You can add flaked almonds to the top about 15 minutes into the cooking time if you like.

Cool on a wire rack with the greaseproof still attached, then wrap in greaseproof and foil and keep for a couple of days before cutting into squares.

CHOCOLATE AND HAZELNUT CAKE

This is a surprisingly subtle and delicious cake, with a toasted hazelnut top, which my cousin Deborah first cooked for me some years ago. I've adapted it minutely, by keeping back some of the chocolate to melt in with the hazelnuts on top. It might appear plain – it absolutely isn't.

Makes an 18cm/7in cake

170g/6oz unsalted butter
170g/6oz light muscovado
   sugar
3 eggs, beaten
2 tbsp milk
170g/6oz wholemeal flour,
   sifted
2½ tsp baking powder
200g/7oz best bitter
   chocolate, chopped quite
   small
110g/4oz ground hazelnuts
30g/1oz chopped hazelnuts

Preheat the oven to 180°C/350°F/Gas 4. Grease and line an 18cm/7in round cake tin. It should be springform so you can cool the cake without having to turn it upside down.

Cream the butter with the sugar until light and fluffy. Add the eggs, a little at a time, beating between each addition. Then fold in the milk, sifted flour and baking powder, mixing them thoroughly. Add about two-thirds of the chopped chocolate, together with the ground hazelnuts, and spoon the mixture into the prepared tin.

Finally, sprinkle the chopped hazelnuts and the remaining chocolate over the mixture and bake in the centre of the oven for about 1½ hours, or until the centre is springy when lightly touched. After the first hour, cover the cake with a sheet of greaseproof paper to prevent the nuts from burning.

Leave to cool slightly in the tin, then carefully release the springform clip and transfer the cake to a wire rack. Best eaten while still warm, with or without cream.

POLENTA, ALMOND AND LEMON CAKE

I have adapted this from the original 'River Café Cook Book'. The golden-crusted cake should ooze a slightly sad, grainy, almondy centre.

Serves 12

340g/12oz unsalted butter, softened
340g/12oz golden caster or icing sugar
340g/12oz organic ground almonds
2 tsp vanilla extract
4 large eggs
zest of 3 lemons and juice of 1 of them
225g/8oz organic polenta
1½ tsp baking powder
½ tsp sea salt

Preheat the oven to 170°C/325°F/Gas 3. Butter and flour a 23cm/9in springform cake tin.

Beat the butter and sugar together in an electric mixer, or by hand, until light and fluffy. Stir in the ground almonds and vanilla. Beat in the eggs, one at a time. Fold in the lemon zest and juice, the polenta, baking powder and salt. Spoon into the cake tin. Bake for an hour, but keep checking from 45 minutes. Delicious with ice cream.

DRENCHED GINGER AND LEMON CAKE

This is my take on the classic lemon cake, whose top you attack with deep skewer holes and trickle down a sticky, tangy lemon syrup. This is the same with ginger and lemon, but the ginger's heat and strength does not overwhelm the citrus. The top ends up looking rather like a glossy, caramel-coloured brandy snap.

Serves 6–8

170g/6oz unsalted butter
170g/6oz light muscovado
   sugar
2 large eggs
grated zest and juice of
   2 lemons
1 tsp baking powder
a pinch of salt
170g/6oz self-raising flour;
   I used ½ Shipton Mill's
   wholemeal, ½ Dove's Farm
   organic plain white
3–5 tbsp milk
4 pieces of ginger from a jar
   of stem ginger in syrup
45g/1½oz demerara sugar
2 tbsp ginger syrup

Preheat the oven to 180°C/350°F/Gas 4. Butter a 15–18cm/6–7in cake tin and line the base with a circle of buttered greaseproof paper. Cream the butter and muscovado sugar until light and fluffy, then beat in the eggs one at a time. Grate the lemon zest into the mixture, then sift over the baking powder, salt and flour and fold them in lightly with a metal spoon. Stir in enough milk to give a dropping consistency, then add the finely chopped ginger and fold in lightly. Plop into the tin, smooth the top, and bake in the centre of the oven for 40–50 minutes, until springy to the touch in the centre.

Remove from the oven, and leave for 15 minutes before turning out on to a rack. When still warm, place on a plate, and with a long skewer, pierce holes all over the cake from the top through to the bottom. Put the demerara sugar, lemon juice and ginger syrup in a pan, stir as it heats to dissolve the sugar, then bubble it up fiercely for a minute or so. Pour it as slowly as you can over the top of the cake, allowing it to seep down the holes.

Serve warm or cold with crème fraîche.

SPICED FRUIT LOAF

A delicious spiced loaf speckled with organic vine fruits, a bit like a giant hot-cross bun. My daughter Charissa's tasting notes for this are as follows, 'Serve thickly coated with butter, and honey if you've got a sweet tooth.'

Makes 2 small loaves

500g/1lb 2oz strong white organic flour, I used Shipton Mill's
a large pinch of salt
30g/1oz fresh yeast, from health food stores or supermarkets with in-store bakeries
1 heaped tsp mixed spice
75g/2½oz non-hydrogenated vegetable spread such as Biona or Suma
roughly 300ml/½ pint water
75g/2½oz organic raisins
55g/2oz each organic currants and sultanas

Sift the flour and salt into a large bowl and crumble in the fresh yeast. Add the mixed spice and the vegetable margarine in small pieces, and work it and the yeast in as you would for a crumble. Work in the water until you have a ball of stiffish dough. Leave it somewhere warm to prove for an hour and double in size, then knock it back with vim and vigour, adding the vine fruits.

Grease a baking sheet lightly with a bit of sunflower oil or the like, divide the dough into two, and put each round ball, like two large rolls, on the baking sheet. Allow to double in size again, about another hour. Preheat the oven to 200°C/400°F/Gas 6 and bake for about 30 minutes. The loaves will be quite dense, with a lightly coloured top. Cool on a wire rack.

ALMOND MACAROON CAKE

When Sally Edwards used to bake this cake at her River Café in Taunton, the strongest-willed non-puddinger would have weakened. It should be eaten with a memory of warmth to it, alongside some spiced plums, apricots or pears. The top should be both crunchy and gooey at the same time.

Serves 6–8

170g/6oz unsalted butter, softened
140g/5oz unrefined vanilla caster sugar
a pinch of salt
zest of an organic lemon
2 organic eggs
4–5 tbsp crème fraîche
140g/5oz unbleached self-raising flour
85g/3oz almonds, freshly ground

Topping

2 egg whites
110g/4oz unrefined vanilla caster sugar
85g/3oz almonds, freshly ground

Preheat the oven to 180°C/350°F/Gas 4. Grease a 15cm/6in cake tin, then place a circle of greased greaseproof paper in the bottom of it. Cream the softened butter and sugar together thoroughly. Add a pinch of salt, the lemon zest and the eggs, one by one, beating as you go. Fold in four tablespoons of crème fraîche, the sifted flour and the almonds. If the mixture is a little heavy, slacken it with another tablespoon of crème fraîche. Bake in the centre of the oven for 30 minutes.

Five minutes before you are due to take the cake out, whisk the whites stiffly, incorporate half the sugar and whisk again until stiff. Fold in the almonds and the rest of the sugar lightly and quickly. Take the cake out of the oven and gently but swiftly pile the macaroon mixture on top and spread it across. Return the cake to the oven for about 20 minutes. The top should be biscuit coloured and crisp to the touch. Cool for 10 minutes, turn out and serve warm with crème fraîche. You can also leave the cake to cool completely, and warm it gently a few hours later when you want to eat it.

5

Saturday supper

Should you follow the long, slow, simple and succulent school of cooking or go for the burn and try a new recipe you've been drooling and deliberating over for an age? Whichever route you take, get the starter made or prepped, whip up a cold pud, give yourself bathing, drinking, talking and relaxing time, and unwind with a great Saturday supper.

LEEKS VINAIGRETTE

A perfect summer starter, with the new season's taut white wands of leek, and that magical combination of chives, mustard and chopped egg. A real classic.

Serves 4

12 fine leeks
2 tbsp Dijon mustard
4 tbsp warm water
2 tbsp red or white wine
  vinegar
150ml/5fl oz olive oil, or more
  to taste
salt and pepper
2 softly hard-boiled organic
  eggs
a handful of snipped chives

Wash the leeks very well and trim the green leaves to about 2.5cm/1in. Steam them until collapsed and tender. Drain and allow them to cool, then halve them lengthwise.

Blitz the mustard, water, vinegar, salt and pepper in a blender, then, with the motor running, gradually pour in the olive oil until you have a thick, mustardy emulsion. Taste and adjust. You might need a little more water if it is too thick. Irrigate the leeks, which you have laid regimental-style in a flat dish, then sprinkle over the finely chopped egg and the snipped chives.

PARMESAN GRISSINI

This is Dan Lepard's version of the chef Giorgio Locatelli's Parmesan grissini.

Makes about 20

120ml/4fl oz full-cream milk
1 tsp dry active yeast
55g/2oz unsalted butter
55g/2oz Parmesan cheese,
   freshly grated
200g/7oz strong white flour
½ tsp fine sea salt

Preheat the oven to 180°C/350°F/Gas 4. Warm the milk until tepid, then whisk in the dried yeast. Melt the butter in a small saucepan over a low heat and pour it into the warm milk. Add the grated Parmesan and stir together, then add the flour and salt and work the mixture until a dough is formed.

Knead lightly for 10–15 seconds; wrap the dough in a damp tea towel and leave for 10 minutes. Knead the dough once more for a further 10–15 seconds, cover again, and leave for 30 minutes. Knead a final time for 10–15 seconds, cover and leave for 45 minutes.

Lightly flour the work surface and roll the dough until it's about 1cm/½in thick. With a sharp knife or pizza cutter and a ruler, cut strips of dough about 1cm/½in wide. Roll each strip into grissini and place them on a non-stick baking sheet. Bake for 15–20 minutes until crisp and lightly golden. Remove from the oven and cool on a wire rack.

RATATOUILLE

There are no short cuts for this classic-for-all-seasons. The secret of the best ratatouille is simple: the vegetables have to be cooked separately before they are married. That way they retain their individual flavour, texture and character. You do not, after all, want an amorphous swamp of bland, over-stewed, oily-puddle-on-a-plate apology for this Mediterranean joy.

Serves 4–6

2 large aubergines
2 red peppers
1 large onion, finely sliced
3 cloves of garlic, chopped
4 courgettes, sliced
1 x 400g/13oz tin plum
    tomatoes or 450g/1lb fresh
    tomatoes, skinned, seeded
    and chopped
a sprig of thyme and a couple
    of bay leaves
a handful of fresh basil
olive oil
sea salt and black pepper

Slice the aubergines into discs, brush them with olive oil and place on baking parchment on a baking sheet. Roast them in a hot oven, 200°C/440°F/Gas 6, until tender, 15–20 minutes. This is quite the best way to cook aubergines without them absorbing barrels of oil.

Meanwhile, put the red peppers on a baking sheet in the oven and turn them every time a side chars, or hold them with a pair of tongs over a naked flame. Put the charred peppers into a plastic bag or a bowl covered with clingfilm for 20 minutes until you can handle them and the steam has eased the skin from the flesh. Peel, core, de-seed and cut them into strips or larger pieces, depending on your preference.

Sauté the onion and garlic gently in a little olive oil until softened. Add the courgettes, thyme, bay leaf and black pepper and a little more oil if necessary. When the courgettes have begun to soften, add the tomatoes and bring to a bubble before adding the aubergines and red peppers. Stew everything gently for a further five to ten minutes. Check the seasoning and leave to cool. Ratatouille is best eaten warm or cold. Strew the torn basil leaves over the top before serving.

SCALLOPS
WITH MINTED PEA PURÉE

The most important thing is the freshness and size of the scallops. My fishmonger, Phil Bowditch, in Taunton, has boats returning the same day the scallops are caught, so they are still alive in the shell. If they are beginning to smell, or look plumped up with water, avoid them. The scallop's sweet fleshiness marries beautifully with sweet legumes – Rowley Leigh cooks a particularly good combination of scallops with minted pea purée.

For the scallops, I use a ridged toasting machine, brushed with a tiny bit of olive oil before heating. You can use a griddle or frying pan, but need to turn the scallops at half time. When the surface is hot, quickly place the white discs of scallop on top. After about a minute, add the coral, close the lid, and wait about another minute. The moment the whites are translucent, they are cooked. Place a heap of pea purée on each plate, with the scallops on top, add the chopped parsley, season and serve.

MINTED PEA PURÉE

Sauté the onion gently in a bit of olive oil until softened and translucent. Add most of the mint, and cook briefly. Add the boiling chicken stock, bring it back to the boil, and pour on the peas, cooking them until they're done. Strain the liquid and reserve. Put the peas in the liquidizer and blend, adding a bit of the stock, but keeping the purée thick. Season with sugar, salt and pepper, and sprinkle over some really finely chopped mint leaves. Serve immediately, so it doesn't lose its green brilliance. Keep the remaining stock for soup.

Serves 6 as a starter

2 large scallops per person,
   cleaned and trimmed,
   the white sliced in two, the
   corals left whole
a knob of butter and olive oil
salt and freshly ground
   pepper
dusting of flat-leaf parsley

Minted pea purée

1 onion, finely chopped
olive oil
a handful of mint
570ml/1 pint good chicken
   stock
1kg/2¼lb frozen peas
sugar, salt and pepper to taste

COLD POACHED SALMON OR SEA TROUT
WITH GRIDDLED ASPARAGUS AND GREEN MAYONNAISE

The method I use of cooking salmon at a very low temperature retains all the moisture and vibrant colour of the fish. I find most people overcook their fish so that the flesh becomes dry and welded to the bones. Gentle poaching in a cool oven in a foil parcel is all a whole fish needs, along with a dollop of the finest home-made mayonnaise, fresh peas or asparagus and waxy new potatoes.

Serves 8

1 wild salmon or sea trout up to 2.25kg/5lb, cleaned and gutted
a bunch of herbs such as chervil, dill and parsley
white wine
olive oil if you are serving the fish cold, butter if hot
sea salt and black pepper

Green mayonnaise

2 egg yolks
170ml/6fl oz of good extra virgin olive oil
1 tbsp each of chervil, parsley and chives
half a lemon
salt and pepper

Preheat the oven to 150°C/300°F/Gas 2. Wash the fish and place it on a large sheet of foil with two foil straps laid across it to make the fish easier to flip on to a serving plate. Stuff it with herbs, then scrunch the ends of the foil together to form a boat so the liquid can't escape.

Splash over some white wine and add a glug of olive oil or smear with butter. Season and press the edges of the foil together so the fish is sealed in a loose parcel.

Place on a baking sheet and cook for one hour. If the fish is slim or weighs nearer the 1.4–1.6kg/3–3½lb mark, 40 minutes should do it, but check with a knife-point that the flesh yields right through to the centre. Cool in the foil parcel if serving cold. Skinning is easier than you'd imagine. You will see a line like a plumb line running the length of the fish. Insert the point of the knife along it, then peel, flipping the fish over to do the other side. Keep the fishy juices to slacken the mayonnaise.

GRIDDLED ASPARAGUS

Allow half a dozen spears per person. Much has been written about steaming asparagus, but if you have a griddle, the texture and intensity of flavour is preserved better.

Snap off the woody bottoms and peel the lower half of each asparagus stem with a potato peeler. Roll the asparagus in a good olive oil. Heat the griddle, then add the asparagus spears.

When they have the customary scorch marks, roll them over and continue to cook until al dente when pierced with a knife. (You may need to pull the tips over the edge of the griddle before the thick ends are cooked through.) Remove with tongs to the plate on which you have placed the fish and spritz with a little lemon and black pepper.

GREEN HERB MAYONNAISE

Stir two egg yolks together in a bowl. Add the olive oil, drip, by drip to begin
with, stirring constantly.

Once you have a solid emulsion, you can add a steady stream of oil without
coming to any grief. Finally, squeeze in the juice of half a lemon, season,
slacken with a few tablespoons of the fish juices and add the herbs.

SMOKED HADDOCK SOUFFLÉ

I always include at least one of my cousin Deborah's recipes in my books. She's one of the best cooks I know and these soufflés are utterly delicious. Surprisingly easy too.

Serves 6

500g/1lb young spinach
500g/1lb undyed smoked
    haddock
290ml/10fl oz full-fat milk
1 bay leaf
10 peppercorns
55g/2oz unsalted butter
55g/2oz plain flour
4 eggs
salt, freshly ground black
    pepper, nutmeg

Preheat the oven to 180°C/350°F/Gas 4. Grease six ramekins. Wash the spinach and steam until just wilted. Drain the spinach well and add some black pepper and a grating of nutmeg. Divide the spinach between the ramekins.

Put the smoked haddock in an ovenproof dish with the milk, peppercorns and bay leaf and poach in the oven for 15 minutes. When the fish is cooked, strain the milk off and put it aside. Make a roux with the butter and flour and add the milk from the fish poaching to make a white sauce. Cook for at least 10 minutes, then season with black pepper. Go easy on the salt as smoked fish carries a lot of it. Flake the cooked fish and add it to the white sauce. Separate the eggs, beat the yolks and add to the fish and sauce.

Turn up the oven to 200°C/400°F/Gas 6. Whisk the egg whites until stiff, but not dry and fold them into the sauce mixture with a metal spoon. Divide the mixture between the ramekins, then run your finger round the top of each one so that the soufflés don't catch when cooking and can rise easily.

Place the ramekins on a baking tray and put into the hot oven. Cook for 30–35 minutes until well risen and brown on the top.

TURBOT
WITH SAUCE VIERGE

The king of fish, turbot needs no more accompaniment than this simple, raw sauce, which is really just a glorious emulsion of a dressing.

Serves 6

1 × 2.25–3kg/5–6½lb turbot
55g/2oz unsalted butter
150ml/5fl oz white wine
a small bunch of chervil and
  flat-leaf parsley, chopped
sea salt and black pepper

Sauce vierge
4 ripe tomatoes, skinned,
  de-seeded and chopped
1 tbsp red wine vinegar
1 clove of garlic, peeled and
  thinly sliced
1 shallot, peeled and very
  finely chopped
salt and black pepper
150ml/5fl oz best olive oil
a small bunch of basil

Stuff the fish with the herbs. Grease a large roasting tin with butter, and place the fish in it. Pour over the white wine, dot the fish with butter and season. Cover the fish with a sheet of greaseproof paper and cook it for about 25 minutes before testing it with a skewer to make sure it is cooked right the way through. How long it will take depends on the thickness of the fish, so if it is only a tiny bit resistant at its thickest point, check it again in five minutes. It is not difficult – fish are not temperamental or more difficult to master than meat, but there is less leeway between being cooked and overcooked.

SAUCE VIERGE
Let the first four ingredients macerate, together with a little salt and a good scrunch of black pepper, for 30 minutes. Stir in the olive oil and add the torn leaves of basil before pouring it over the warm, poached fish.

VITELLO TONNATO
WITH GREEN OLIVES

A classic summer dish, relying on an olive oil-based mayonnaise for strength of flavour, that can be made, unbelievably, up to five days before you want to eat it. I do not, as is conventional, poach the veal. I roast it.

Serves 8

1kg/2¼lb boned loin of veal
1 onion, finely sliced
flat-leaf parsley

Fresh tuna sauce

225g/8oz tuna steak
6 anchovy fillets
3 tbsp capers, drained
3 tbsp lemon juice
240ml/8fl oz olive oil
salt, pepper
12–15 green olives, stoned
  and roughly chopped
mayonnaise, made with 2 egg
  yolks, 290ml/10fl oz olive
  oil, the juice of a lemon and
  salt and pepper

Grill or griddle the tuna steak until just tender, about two to three minutes. Process all the tuna sauce ingredients, bar the mayonnaise and the green olives, until creamy and smooth, but do not overdo it. Stir in the green olives, then fold in the mayonnaise.

Roast the veal for an hour on a finely sliced onion in a hottish oven, 190°C/375°F/Gas 5. Cool, slice and add the warm meat juices to the tuna sauce. Spread a layer of tuna sauce thinly on a serving dish, top with slices of veal, spread another layer of sauce, and repeat until the final layer of sauce.

Scatter some chopped, flat-leaf parsley over the top, and decorate sparingly with a few anchovy fillets and black olives. Refrigerate for at least 24 hours.

DAUBE OF PORK
WITH APRICOTS

I have eaten a 'white' daube several times at Lindsay House, the Soho restaurant of my favourite chef, Richard Corrigan. He understands the cheaper cuts of meat better anyone else I know, potting, curing, brining from snout to tail the cuts that many people reject nowadays, mostly out of the combined qualities of shameful ignorance and a feeling that anything that requires longer, slower cooking requires, absurdly, longer, slower preparation. Total myth. Pork shoulder, like shoulder of lamb, wins for taste over leg every day in my book, and lends itself perfectly to the gentle braise that should be at the heart of winter cooking. The sharpness of the apricots – I use unsulphured sticky dark ones, Richard doesn't, he goes for colour – is an inspired touch over the more traditional use of prunes, a sweeter cousin. My interpretation of Richard's dish is just that, a bit of guesswork and poetic licence. If you want to eat the real thing, go to the restaurant.

Serves 8

1 shoulder of pork, about
   1.5 kg/ 3¼lb
3 organic unsulphured
   apricots per person
freshly squeezed orange juice
white wine
olive oil
2.5 litres/4½ pints of veal
   stock, failing that beef stock

Marinade

1 tbsp cumin seeds
½ tbsp fennel seeds
85g/3oz runny honey
100ml/3½fl oz red wine
   vinegar
8 cloves of garlic
4 sprigs of thyme, the leaves
   pulled from the stems
500ml/18fl oz red wine
5 sprigs of mint, finely
   chopped
the zest of an organic orange
sea salt and black pepper

Preheat the oven to 170°C/325°F/Gas 3. Soak the apricots in an equal amount of orange juice and sweet white wine to cover.

Remove the rind of the pork and cut the meat into 110g/4oz pieces. Mix the marinade ingredients together in a large bowl. Add the meat, mixing everything together well with your fingers, cover the bowl and put it in the fridge for 24 hours. Remove the meat and pat it dry with kitchen paper, then brown it in batches in olive oil in a large heavy-bottomed casserole. Remove it to a plate.

Pour the marinade and meat juices into the casserole and reduce over a high heat to about half their original volume. Return the meat to the pot, cover it with the veal stock, a sheet of greaseproof paper and a lid and cook for two hours in the oven.

Meanwhile, gently cook the apricots in their marinade until soft but still holding their shape, and add them to the pork at the end of cooking.

Mashed potato, briefly cooked, and refreshed buttered cabbage, perhaps a baked onion, what more could you want?

CHICKEN SAVOYARDE

There are dishes whose pedigree is so unimpeachable you cannot alter them one iota; they are true thoroughbreds. This particular one came into my hands through two generations of top-drawer cooks, Tim Withers of The George and Dragon at Rowde in Wiltshire, whose dish it is, via the illustrious chef and food writer Simon Hopkinson. As Simon has noted, '50 grams of tarragon may seem a lot but, believe me, it makes all the difference.' I cannot implore you enough to try this dish: it is as good as it gets and there is no difficulty in its execution. Even if there were, it would be worth it. Suitable for your most serious or celebratory of occasions.

Serves 6

1 x 2kg/4½lb organic chicken
2 onions, peeled, one of them
  stuck with 2 cloves
2 carrots, peeled and sliced in
  half lengthways
3 sticks of celery, chopped in
  half
2 leeks, trimmed and well
  washed
2 bay leaves and 2 sprigs of
  thyme
salt

Sauce and to finish

55g/2oz butter
55g/2oz flour
400ml/14fl oz poaching stock
300ml/10½fl oz dry white
  wine
240ml/8fl oz double cream
100g/3½oz Gruyère cheese,
  grated
1 tbsp Dijon mustard
55g/2oz tarragon leaves,
  chopped
salt and pepper
55g/2oz breadcrumbs
30g/1oz Parmesan cheese,
  grated

Put the chicken into a large pot, add the vegetables, herbs and salt. Poach very gently for around an hour and a half, skimming off any scum that comes to the surface. Once cooked, lift out the bird and allow to cool. Strain the stock through a fine sieve and discard all solids. Leave to settle and lift off any surface fat using several sheets of absorbent kitchen paper.

Remove all the meat from the chicken carcass (discarding skin and also removing all sinews from the drumsticks) and cut into large, bite-sized pieces.

To make the sauce, melt the butter in a pan, add the flour and cook for three minutes without browning. Gradually add the hot chicken stock, white wine and cream and stir until thickened. Stir in the cheese, mustard and tarragon, correct the seasoning and simmer all together for about 20 minutes.

Preheat the oven to 230°C/450°F/Gas 8. Put the chicken in a buttered gratin dish, pour over the sauce and sprinkle with the breadcrumbs and Parmesan cheese. Bake for 20–25 minutes until the dish is golden brown and bubbling well around the edges. Eat with buttered new potatoes and a crisp green salad.

COQ AU VIN

I have a sense that this classic dish has fallen from grace, but it is just the kind of food I love. My children agree. As with all classics, they should never be downgraded by the use of inferior ingredients, or by missing out things like the Cognac! Aim for a sauce that coats the fowl with a gluey, ruby-red richness and depth of flavour. Either use a whole, jointed organic chicken, or, as I did, six good-sized legs.

Serves 6

1 whole organic chicken, jointed or 6 good-sized legs
85g/3oz unsalted butter
3 tbsp olive oil
110g/4oz organic green back bacon, diced
18 shallots, but who's counting, peeled and left whole
4 whole cloves of garlic
18 organic mushrooms, halved
flour
a bouquet of fresh thyme, flat-leaf parsley and bay
4 tbsp Cognac
1 bottle full-bodied red wine
1 tsp molasses sugar
salt and pepper
1 tbsp each of butter and flour
a handful of flat-leaf parsley

Preheat the oven to 180°C/350°F/Gas 5. Heat the butter and olive oil in a heavy-bottomed casserole, and throw in the bacon. Sauté briefly, then add the shallots, garlic and mushrooms and cook gently until the shallots are beginning to turn opaque and pale gold. Remove with a slatted spoon, and add the chicken pieces that you have shaken with some seasoned flour in a ziploc bag, then shaken the excess flour from. Brown first on one side then the other, for five minutes a side. Return the bacon and vegetables to the pot, add the bouquet and season, before covering with a lid and cooking until tender, about 25 minutes.

Set a saucepan on top of the stove on a moderate heat, warm the Cognac in a ladle, then pour it into the pan and set it alight. Let the alcohol burn off before adding the heated red wine and a teaspoon of molasses sugar. Reduce by about a third, then thicken with some old-fashioned beurre manie made with a tablespoon each of butter and flour. Strain the sauce into the coq and keep hot until ready to serve. Scatter with chopped parsley.

CHICKEN STEWED
WITH CARROTS AND MOROCCAN SPICES TO COME

I served this spicy chicken dish with couscous (cooked according to the packet instructions), into which I had added six cardamom pods, a stick of cinnamon, three cloves and a teaspoon of allspice. I toasted a handful of pine nuts and forked them into the couscous with a handful of raisins. Do give the the harissa with crushed rose petals a try — I like the Belazu brand, available in Sainsbury's Special Selection.

Serves 6

6 organic chicken legs or thighs
450g/1lb carrots, sliced into coins,
8 cloves garlic
olive oil
3 red onions
sprig each of rosemary, thyme, parsley
3 bay leaves
½ tsp each cinnamon, cloves, ginger and allspice
1½ tsp each cumin and coriander, dry roasted in a pan for 30 seconds and ground
1 tsp paprika
a glass of Marsala
1 tbsp harissa with crushed rose petals
a handful of flat-leaf parsley and/or coriander

Preheat the oven to 150°C/300°F/Gas 2. Simmer the carrots with two cloves of peeled garlic, 240ml/8fl oz of water and 4 tablespoons of olive oil until cooked through. Brown the chicken on all sides in a heavy-bottomed pan in a little olive oil. Remove the chicken to a plate and gently sauté the onions until softened in the oil and chicken fat, adding the rest of the garlic, thickly chopped, halfway through. Add the finely chopped herbs, bay leaves and spices.

Return the chicken to the pan, add the Marsala and its equivalent in water and the harissa, stir and bring to the bubble. Cover with a sheet of greaseproof and a lid and cook in the oven for 40–45 minutes, testing with a skewer to make sure the juices run clear. About 15 minutes before the end of cooking time, tip in the cooked carrots and continue to cook.

At the end of cooking, strew some more fresh parsley and/or coriander over the dish. Serve with some more harissa on the side for those who like things hot.

LAMB SHANKS BRAISED
WITH BALSAMIC VINEGAR AND WHITE WINE

Richard Corrigan and I cooked this together, keeping the onions and garlic whole so they could be eaten as a vegetable, melted down into the velvety balsamic vinegar and herbs. We both think that shanks work better with white wine than red.

Serves 4

4 lamb shanks
a ziploc bag containing
  4 tbsp flour and some sea
  salt and black pepper
3 tbsp olive oil
a knob of butter
4 large onions, skinned and
  almost quartered, so they
  don't separate from the
  root end
a head of new season's garlic,
  skinned
a bouquet of rosemary,
  thyme, bay and parsley tied
  together
240ml/8fl oz dry white wine
150ml/5fl oz well-aged,
  mellow balsamic vinegar
a couple of strips of lemon
  peel

Throw the shanks into the bag, seal it and toss them around until they are coated in seasoned flour, then shake off the excess. Heat the oil and butter in a heavy-bottomed pot, and brown the lamb shanks all over.

Remove to a plate, add a little more oil and fat to the pot if you need to, and add the onions, garlic and herbs. Sauté gently until opaque and golden, then raise the heat and add the wine and vinegar. Let everything bubble for two minutes to burn off the alcohol.

Return the shanks to the pan, add the lemon strips, tuck a layer of greaseproof paper over them and cover with a lid. Simmer very gently for 1½–2 hours, but check after 1½ hours.

STEAK

STEAK IS FOOD for when you've been getting physical – and I'm not just talking leisurely strokes on the tennis court. First, find your appetite; second, sort out your technique; and third, remember that if it's not well hung, it won't do it for you.

So what should you buy and how should you cook it? Fillet is flavourless, but people buy it because they know they can't go wrong with it. It's hard to make it tough, because it comes from a muscle underneath the ribcage that never does any work. It has neither the fat nor the flavour, which develop when the muscle is used.

What about rib-eye? Charlotte Reynolds, of Swaddles Green Farm, at Chard in Somerset, thinks it's as good as rump. 'It's a continuation of the sirloin', she says. 'Where the sirloin ends, it becomes fore-rib; and the rib-eye is the core of the fore-rib. It's where the weight of the animal is carried and where the legs work. It's very well marbled – the most marbled of all the steaks.'

This is the steak best suited to barbecuing, because the marbling acts like a baster. 'The fibres lie the same way as on a fillet steak, so you can cut straight across it', Reynolds adds. 'Rib-eye is loose-textured compared to rump, so it's more tender, but equals it in flavour. In the rump there are several muscles going in different directions, so you always have to cut at right angles to the direction of the grain. Sirloin steak is dense, muscley and full of flavour. It's more tender than rump, but similar in flavour – and with more marbling.'

Breeding is important. Reynolds's beef is from native British breeds: Red Devons, Galloways, Shorthorns and Sussex. Hanging is critical, too: ask your butcher for a three-week minimum. This is something you're unlikely to find in a supermarket, where animals are cut into 'primals', the big main joints, then matured in vacuum packs. Without hanging and drying on the bone, the meat is bound not to taste so good. The darker hued and more marbled the meat, the better; because it is older and has been hung longer.

Steak is expensive, but there are some great cuts of beef that are both cheap and tender. What we call skirt (the French call it 'onglet' or 'bavette') is wonderful if cooked briefly at a high temperature and sliced paper-thin across the grain (long cooking renders it tough). Or a joint of rolled brisket can be slow-roasted in a pot with white wine and herbs. Eat it hot from the pot or cool it, slice it and serve with a green sauce of summer herbs, cornichons, vinegar and horseradish.

Cooking steak is all about going against the grain, perfecting your technique, and buying the right meat for the job. Top rump or back rib are not equal to it. They will give you serious grief if you whack them, short-order style, on a hot griddle or barbecue. If you must use top rump, bash it senseless into minute steaks. Otherwise go for rib-eye, rump or sirloin.

Don't spike the meat with a meat blade: this sends a rash of blood to the surface, drying the meat and making you think your steak is undercooked. Touch is the answer when cooking steak. As the heat penetrates the meat, the muscles stiffen; so if you lay a finger on the surface of rare meat, it will feel soft, because the fibres haven't fused yet. As you cook the meat longer, it will become firmer. Medium-rare will be slightly resistant to the touch; well-done will feel quite hard.

STEAK
WITH BEARNAISE SAUCE

If you like your meat blue, don't rest it. It will merely need a minute a side at a very high temperature to char the outside. (The interior will not be cooked, however, so make sure to start with the meat at room temperature.) Otherwise, it is extremely important to rest the meat to allow the heat to warm the blood in the middle of the steak. A good butcher will cut a steak about 2cm/¾in thick.

Serves 6

1 steak per person, 2cm/¾in
    thick
sea salt, black pepper
olive oil

Bearnaise sauce
2 tbsp white wine vinegar
    (or tarragon vinegar)
3 tbsp finely snipped French
    tarragon
30g/1oz finely chopped
    shallot
10 peppercorns, crushed
4 egg yolks
3 tbsp cold water
225g/8oz clarified unsalted
    butter
sea salt and freshly ground
    black pepper
2 tbsp finely chopped chervil
    (optional)
juice of half a lemon

To cook the steak, first season the meat with sea salt and cracked pepper. If you are using a griddle or pan, rather than a barbecue, brush it with a little olive oil as it gets hot. Heat until smoking before adding the meat. For a rare steak, cook for two minutes a side, then rest it for six minutes. For medium rare, cook for 2½ minutes a side, then rest it for five minutes. For well done, cook for five minutes a side and don't rest it at all.

BEARNAISE SAUCE
Put the vinegar, 2 tablespoons of tarragon, shallot and crushed peppercorns in a small, heavy-bottomed saucepan and reduce gently by a half.

Let it cool, add the egg yolks and cold water and set the pan over a low heat, whisking continuously. The sauce will gradually emulsify – be patient, it will take about 10 minutes. Do not allow it to reach boiling point.

Remove from the heat and whisk in the butter a little at a time. Season, then sieve the sauce and stir in the third tablespoon of tarragon, the chervil and the lemon juice to taste. Serve immediately. Good crusty bread is also delicious dipped into Bearnaise sauce.

INSTANT NELLIE MELBA SYLLABUB

There has been much written about syllabub and the importance of steeping the alcohol, lemon and sugar overnight for the flavours to mingle and marry. But sometimes one is in a hurry. I have made two instant versions of this dish. If the cream is chilled when you start and you return the whole to the fridge for 30 minutes, it works delectably. Even if you don't dissolve the sugar in the alcohol properly and end up with a slightly crunchy syllabub, it is still the most poetic of puddings.

Serves 6

2 white peaches, skinned
4 tbsp raspberries and extra
    to decorate
2 tbsp blueberries

Syllabub

2 tbsp Oloroso or good dry
    sherry
1 tbsp Cognac (a good one
    such as Rémy Martin if
    possible)
finely grated zest and juice of
    a lemon
1–2 tbsp vanilla caster sugar
425ml/15fl oz double cream,
    unpasteurized Jersey if
    possible

In a bowl, measure the alcohols and add the zest and juice of the lemon and the sugar. Stir so the sugar begins to dissolve. Pour in the double cream and beat with a balloon whisk until the mixture holds, but not rigidly so.

Cut two ripe peaches, white if possible, into slices. Put a layer of flavoured cream into each glass, add a layer of peach slices, then repeat the cream and add a spoonful of berries. Finish with berries and a final spoon of cream and then put three or four raspberries or blueberries on top before refrigerating.

PINEAPPLE AND WALNUT UPSIDE-DOWN CAKE

This pineapple cake looks beautiful and tastes refreshingly good. It is as delicious for tea as it is for pudding and can be eaten warm or cold. Use a normal gratin dish, or pudding dish, to bake it in — I used a rectangular terracotta dish measuring about 35 x 25cm/14 x 10in. If you prefer, use half walnuts and half almonds.

Serves 6

1 large pineapple
55g/2oz unsalted butter
55g/2oz light muscovado sugar
225g/8oz unsalted butter, softened
4 large eggs
225g/8oz unrefined granulated sugar
200g/7oz self-raising flour
2 tsp baking powder
55g/2oz walnuts, coarsely ground

Peel the pineapple to remove all the little brown sharp bits. Slice in circles and remove the cores with an apple corer.

Melt the 55g/2oz of butter and muscovado sugar together, then bubble them up, stirring as you go, until they are well amalgamated. Pour this mixture over the bottom of the dish and brush it up the sides. It will drop back into the base, but don't worry.

Put a layer of whole fresh pineapple slices over the mixture in the middle of the dish (mine took three). Cut the rest of the pineapple into semicircles and arrange them down the sides. I fill in the joins with pineapple triangles as I like the cake to be as fruity as possible.

Process the 225g/8oz of butter, eggs, sugar, flour, baking powder and walnuts together and pour them over the pineapple. Bake for 50–60 minutes, checking with a skewer after 50. The top will be golden brown.

Cool to warm, then run a knife around the edge of the cake and turn it upside down on to a plate, where the pineapple will be glazed with a gorgeous butterscotch goo.

Serve with or without cream and a pineapple syrup made with extra pineapple juice and sugar.

STRAWBERRY GENOISE

This is an airily light sponge with a seam of strawberries cooked into it. When you turn it out, it is mottled red and yellow, the fruit bleeding into the sponge.

Makes a 23cm/9 inch cake

4 organic eggs
110g/4oz vanilla caster sugar
rind of an orange
110g/4oz organic flour
a pinch of salt
55g/2oz melted butter
285g/10oz strawberries
1 dsrtsp sugar

Preheat the oven to 180°C/350°F/Gas 4. Brush melted butter over the base and sides of a 23cm/9in springform cake tin. Cover the base with a circle of baking parchment or greaseproof, also buttered, and sprinkle flour over it, shaking off the excess.

Beat the eggs, sugar and rind together until trebled in volume, light and foamy. The beaters will leave a trail. I did it in the KitchenAid, otherwise beat over a pan of barely simmering water, and when expanded, remove and beat until cool.

Sift half the flour on to the egg mixture and fold it in gently with a metal spoon. Sift over the rest of the flour and the salt, then pour the warm butter, without its white sediment, around the side, and fold them all in thoroughly but lightly.

Pour half the mixture into the tin, throw in the strawberries and sprinkle them with a dessertspoon of sugar, then cover with the other half of the mixture. Bake for about 40 minutes. The top should spring back to the touch when cooked. Cool for ten minutes, then turn out on to a wire rack. The strawberries will be uppermost.

CARAMEL AND CHOCOLATE FUDGE CAKE

The first time I made this sensationally rich, dark, flourless cake it was a little too bitter. Second time around I used a mix of chocolates containing 70 per cent and 50 per cent cocoa solids.

Serves 8

340g/12oz/ unrefined caster
  sugar
285g/10oz unsalted butter,
  cut into cubes and chilled
450g/1lb good chocolate,
  melted
6 large eggs, separated
sprinkling of cocoa powder,
  sifted

Preheat the oven to 180°C/350°F/Gas 4. Grease and line a 25cm/10in springform cake tin.

Use a clean saucepan to caramelize the caster sugar with 2 tbsp water (to help avoid crystallization). Try to reach a dark caramel colour without burning the sugar, so watch carefully, and don't stir – although you may move the pan.

Remove from the heat and add the cubes of chilled butter, carefully but quickly, to arrest the caramelization. Stir with a whisk. Add the melted chocolate, whisking constantly, then the six egg yolks, which you must whisk in really well, one at a time, to stop the mixture from splitting. Let the mixture cool to room temperature.

Whisk the egg whites until stiff. Stir in the first tablespoon of whisked egg white, then fold the remaining whites gently and lightly into the mixture. Pour the mixture into the tin and bake for about an hour, until a skewer comes out almost clean. The cake should still be slightly wet inside.

Let the cake cool totally before removing it from the tin and dusting the top with cocoa powder.

VANILLA ICE CREAM

Everyone else removes the vanilla pod at the last moment or sieves the grainy bits out if they've cooked them in. I make no apologies for doing neither. I scoop the seeds out of the pod, cook them in the cream and leave them in, making the rich cream speckledy.

Serves 6 if the only pudding or up to 10 if accompanying another pudding

1 vanilla pod
285ml/10fl oz organic single cream
4 egg yolks, beaten
vanilla caster sugar (sugar that has been stored with a vanilla pod) to taste
285ml/10fl oz organic double cream

Scoop out the seeds from the vanilla pod by cutting all along the pod with a knife, then firmly insert a teaspoon and pull it along the length of the pod. Put the contents of the spoon into a saucepan with the single cream, and bring just to boiling point. Remove from the heat and leave to infuse for 10–15 minutes. Pour the mixture on to the egg yolks, whisk together and return to the pan. Stir gently, or whisk, over a low heat, until the mixture has thickened perceptibly and coats a spoon. Don't try to hurry this by turning up the heat or the mixture will curdle.

Sweeten to taste with vanilla sugar and leave to cool. Whisk the double cream until stiff, pour in the vanilla mixture and fold in gently until thoroughly amalgamated. Freeze.

GOOSEBERRY FOOL

No summer is complete without a summer pudding, a strawberry tart, a cherry pie, Eton mess and a gooseberry fool. Gooseberry fool is my favourite, and to my mind the home-made custard version surpasses the floppily whipped cream version. Rich it is, but that didn't stop the young people of Northamptonshire, according to Kettner's 'Book of the Table' published in 1877. 'After eating as much as they possibly can of this gooseberry fool, they used to roll down a hill and begin eating again.' More fool them.

Serves 4–6

about 450g/1lb/ tart
   gooseberries, topped and
   tailed
55g/2oz unsalted butter
4 tbsp or so muscovado sugar
290ml/½ pint single cream, or
   half each single and double
3 egg yolks
2–3 tbsp elderflower syrup
   (optional)

Elderflower syrup
6 heads of elderflowers
290ml/½ pint water
3 tbsp vanilla caster sugar

To make elderflower syrup, simmer the flowers with the water and sugar for 15 minutes. Leave to infuse under a lid before straining through a sieve.

Stew the gooseberries gently in the melted butter and sugar in a heavy-bottomed frying-pan, turning frequently as the sugar begins to coat and caramelize. Do not allow the berries to overcook. They are cooked when you can crush them with a fork without resistance. Leave them to cool.

Scald the cream in a small pan, then pour it over the beaten egg yolks, whisking as you go, before returning the mixture to the pan. Continue to cook and stir or whisk over a gentle heat until the custard has thickened. Pay attention at this stage or the mixture will scramble.

If you're using the elderflower syrup, stir it into the fruit purée first, then fold the fruit into the custard. Cool and spoon into glasses or a glass bowl. Top with a sprig of redcurrants or a twist of lemon peel to add colour.

Serve chilled with home-made macaroons.

ALMOND MACAROONS

Serves 8

100g/3½oz ground almonds
1 heaped tsp cornflour
2 egg whites
squeeze of lemon juice
pinch of salt
200g/7oz caster sugar
cocoa powder

Preheat the oven to 190°C/375°F/Gas 5. To make the macaroons, sift the ground almonds with the cornflour, then set aside. Whisk the egg whites, lemon and salt until frothy, add a third of the sugar, whisk until soft peak stage; add a third more sugar, whisk until glossy and thick; add the final third of sugar, whisk until stiff peaks form. Fold in the almonds. Spoon or pipe the mixture on to a tray covered with baking parchment. Leave for 20 minutes to dry slightly, put in the oven and turn down the heat to 130°C/ 250°F/Gas ½. Bake until off-white and slightly dry, 15–20 minutes. Cool.

ORANGE-SCENTED RICOTTA CAKE

This is the lightest of cakes, made with potato flour, the ricotta sieved to aerate it. I add a touch of Grand Marnier and orange flower water to the mixture, and serve it alongside strawberries and clotted cream in the summer.

Serves 8

85g/3oz unsalted butter
140g/5oz vanilla caster sugar
2 large organic eggs
grated rinds of half an organic orange and lemon
3 tbsp potato flour
1½ tsp baking powder
pinch of salt
450g/1lb ricotta, if you are lucky enough to find fresh, drain it through a muslin-lined sieve overnight
55g/2oz organic raisins soaked in a little hot water for 15 minutes to plump up
2–3 tsp orange flower water
2 tbsp Grand Marnier or Cointreau
icing sugar

Preheat the oven to 180°C/350°F/Gas 4. Beat the butter and all but a tablespoon of the sugar together until pale and creamy, then add the eggs and continue to whisk. Add the orange and lemon zests, potato flour, baking powder and salt. Push the ricotta through the small disc of a mouli or sieve, and blend it into the other ingredients. Fold in the raisins in their orange brew, and sprinkle over the orange flower water and Grand Marnier.

Butter a 23cm/9in springform tin, then scatter the rest of the sugar into it and roll it around the base and sides, discarding any extra. Scrape in the cake mixture, and bake in the middle of the oven for 55 minutes, or until a skewer comes out clean. Leave to cool.

Turn out on to a plate and sprinkle over a tiny bit of unrefined icing sugar if you like. This is a habit that I refuse to get into – it is so overworked on restaurant puddings, alongside sprigs of this and that and solitary fanned fruit. If in doubt, leave well alone.

QUINCE AND PRALINÉED ALMOND ICE CREAM

This is how the best things in my cooking life come to pass. My great friend George Morley was down for our usual greedy guzzlers weekend with her husband Shawn and son Charlie. We were deliberating whether to make a torta di Santiago with the membrillo (quince paste) we had. Laziness won the day. She suggested it would be quicker to make a membrillo ice cream. I suggested we should keep the Spanish influence and add Oloroso and pralinéed almonds as the torta would have been rich with Valencia almonds. We stirred and squeezed and melted and ground, eating many of the pralinéed almonds before they got anywhere near the ice cream. This was the result, judged, in our rather unhumble opinions, to be one of our fairer and more delectable creations!

Serves 4–6

225g/8oz membrillo (quince paste, sold in good supermarkets and by mail order from Roberts and Speight 01482 870717)
2 tbsp lemon juice
1 tbsp water
1 tbsp Oloroso or other sherry
290ml/½ pint double cream, Jersey if possible
140g/5oz almonds (ideally Valencia), whole but blanched (sold in good supermarkets)
55–85g/2–3oz unrefined caster sugar

Melt the membrillo gently in a pan with the lemon juice, water and sherry. Whisk the cream until it holds softly, but isn't stiff.

In a non-stick frying pan over a gentle heat, scatter the almonds in a single layer and pour the sugar over them. Stir as the sugar melts and the brittle turns the colour of butterscotch, but not dark brown. Remove from the heat instantly and pour on to a greased baking tray. Leave to solidify, then bash into small chunks and little shards.

Fold the cream into the membrillo mixture, then fold about a third of the brittle into it, and freeze. Remove to the fridge for 30 minutes before serving and offer a bowl of the remaining brittle to scatter sparingly over the top.

6

Sunday lunch

I still find it hard to believe that there are people who don't roast on Sundays, either for lunch or dinner. Perhaps it is because if I didn't, my children would instantly mutiny. Fluffing up parboiled potatoes, pouring batter on to smoking beef dripping, salting a creamy curd of pork fat, pouring the meat juices, wine and vegetable water into the blackened onions on the roasting tin for gravy — that is what Sundays are REALLY about.

A HOME-MADE BLOODY MARY

Why? Because it's worth it. And don't say a Bloody Mary isn't a starter. It's the best precursor to a fine sirloin of beef with the undercut I know, and it is my pre-Sunday lunch, post run-and-bath ritual, which I would have to be shaken not stirred out of to consider giving up. Once you have made the real McCoy you will never go back to your old habits. If you have a pretty glass jug, put it in the deep freeze for 30 minutes before you make your Bloody Mary, and also the glasses if you have room. That way, everything has a rime of frosting when you serve it, quite beautiful.

Makes 6–8 glasses

1kg/2¼lb ripe organic
  tomatoes
2 small stalks of celery from
  the heart, with their leaves
a small bunch of fresh
  coriander
a sprig each of thyme, flat-leaf
  parsley and rosemary
1 tsp grated horseradish, or a
  proprietary brand that is
  pure horseradish
1 tsp grated onion
juice of 2 lemons
a pinch of molasses sugar
a pinch of sea salt
 a few drops each of Tabasco
  and Worcestershire sauce
vodka, about a third of a
  bottle for this quantity
  should do
half a tray of ice cubes

Cut the tomatoes into halves or quarters, depending on their size. Liquidize everything but the alcohol in the food processor or blender, then push as much as you can through a sieve into a bowl, forcing it down hard with the back of a wooden spoon. Pour the cold vodka into the cold jug, add the contents of the bowl and mix well. Adjust the seasoning and serve the Bloody Mary in cold glasses.

If there are any would-be virgins among you, keep back some of the Virgin Mary before you jug it and add the vodka.

CHILLED CRAB, CUCUMBER AND AVOCADO SALAD

I think crab is at its best served chilled, but not icy cold. It is rich though, and you do not need a huge amount of it. The crab that I picked for this dish yielded 340g / 12oz of brown meat and a little less of white, enough for four.

Serves 4

1.5kg/3¼lb crab, cooked
2 ripe Hass avocados
a cucumber
a mixed bag of herbs, ideally a
   tbsp of each of the
   following: chervil, dill and
   chives
2 limes
a few bunches of watercress
   and some rocket or the
   heart of a cos lettuce

Make a dressing with a dessertspoon of home-made mayonnaise, a teaspoon of seeded mustard, a tablespoon of cider vinegar and four or five tablespoons of your best olive oil. Then sieve a couple of tablespoons of the brown crab meat into it and season to taste. You might like to add a tiny pinch of cayenne instead of black pepper.

Put the white crab meat on to a plate with the salad leaves. Add long slivers of avocado and chunks of peeled, seeded cucumber, the finely chopped herbs, and a few quarters of lime to squeeze on. Pour over the dressing, and serve the salad with a loaf of good country bread.

LEG OF LAMB BRAISED SLOWLY
WITH HARICOT BEANS

This is for an older leg, a hogget rather than a tasteless and underage youth, or indeed for a real oldster –
a ruby-red leg of mutton, which Somerset Lamb Direct rear and will send to you in the post.

Serves 8

1 leg of lamb (contact
   Somerset Lamb on
   01398 371387)
500g/1lb 2oz haricot or
   flageolet beans, soaked
   overnight
butter and olive oil
a small ladleful of brandy
225g/8oz unsmoked streaky
   bacon, snipped into strips,
   rind removed
2 carrots, peeled and diced
2 stalks of celery, peeled and
   sliced
2 onions, peeled and chopped
3 leeks, cleaned and sliced
12 whole cloves of garlic,
   peeled
a bunch of fresh rosemary,
   thyme and bay tied together
½ bottle white wine
900ml–1.5 litres/1¾–3 pints
   chicken stock
sea salt and black pepper

Preheat the oven to 230°C/450°F/Gas 8. Drain the beans, just cover them
with fresh water, and bring them to the boil. Remove any scum with a slotted
spoon and kitchen paper, then simmer for an hour. They will be undercooked.
Drain them but keep their liquor.

Heat a knob of butter and a good slug of olive oil in a large, heavy-
bottomed pot. Season, then gently brown the joint on all sides. Pour the
brandy into the pot, warm it, then set light to it with a taper, letting it flame
and crackle until the alcohol has burnt off.

Put the joint and all the juices into a roasting tin. Add a bit more fat and oil
to the pot and brown the bacon, adding the vegetables and garlic when the fat
begins to run. When the vegetables have began to soften, scrape the contents of
the pot into the roasting tin. Add the bouquet of herbs, beans, and enough wine
and stock, which you have heated together, to cover the vegetables but not the
meat. Add some of the bean liquor if you need to.

Cover the tin with foil and cook in the oven for 3½ to 4 hours, turning
every 40 minutes or so. Adjust the seasoning and cut the lamb into thick slices,
heaping each plate with mashed potato, vegetables, beans and juices as you go.

ROAST BONED LEG OF PORK
WITH A SPICED ORANGE RUB AND ORANGE SWEET POTATOES

I rarely cook boned roast meat. There is an expression, 'the nearer the bone, the sweeter the meat' and, of course, the better the flavour. But opening out a joint of lamb or pork when the bone has been removed, flavouring it with something quite other, or piling it full of stuffing, is a different thing altogether, and can be a lovely variant to the standard Sunday roast. Pork marries beautifully with the digestif of a herb marinade. Fennel seed, star anise, dill seed, Pernod and oily orange zest work harmoniously together, particularly if rubbed well into the meat and allowed to penetrate for some time. If you possibly can, buy Middle White or Large Black organic pork, both of which lay down a thick coating of ivory fat. The meat is a superb texture if properly hung and the flavour unlike anything you're likely to get from a newer, faster-reared breed.

Serves 8

2kg/4½lb boned leg of pork,
   untied
1 onion, sliced
sweet potatoes, 1 per person
   depending on size

Marinade

2 tsp fennel seeds
3 star anise
1 tsp dill seeds
sea salt and black pepper
2 crushed fresh bay leaves
a handful of fresh dill,
   chopped
zest of 2 organic oranges
olive oil
2 tbsp Pernod

If you can start preparing this the night before, do; the maceration will tenderize and flavour more deeply. Crush the fennel seeds coarsely with the star anise, dill seeds, sea salt, black peppercorns and bay in a mortar, then add the fresh dill and orange zest and stir in two or three tablespoons of olive oil. Rub the paste well into the opened-out pork where the bone has been removed and all over the outside of the meat and into the crevices where the crackling has been slashed. Not easy, but pull it apart and try and push the paste into the gaps. Concentrate on the inside of the joint, the crackling, and the ends. Splosh on a bit of Pernod and leave covered and in the fridge overnight or for as long as you've got.

Preheat the oven to 200°C/400°F/Gas 6. Bring the meat to room temperature before you roll it up and tie it with string at 2.5cm/1in intervals. Place the joint on top of a sliced onion in a roasting tin. Sprinkle some sea salt over the crackling and put it in the oven. After 40 minutes, baste and turn the oven down to 190°C/375°F/Gas 5.

When the joint has been cooking for about an hour, chop each sweet potato, unskinned, into two or three pieces, roll in the fat surrounding the meat and cook with the joint for 40 minutes, turning them over at half time. The pork will need to rest uncovered for 20 minutes. Do not cover it, or you will jeopardize the brittle, mahogany-coloured crackling.

ROAST CHINED LOIN OF PORK
WITH BAKED APPLES AND CIDER GRAVY

If you don't already know about this cut of meat, I suggest you become acquainted with it. It is the perfect cut when you want to lavish on your guests or family something seriously uncheffy, but stunning, for lunch or dinner. You can scythe through the chines with a flourish, giving everyone a springy, juicy, thick white loin chop on the bone. Next to it, sit a whole baked apple, which you have cored and scored around its circumference and stewed in the fatty juices from the meat and some tartly dry cider.

Serves 6

2kg/4½lb chined loin of organic pork, preferably from an old breed with a good fat covering, such as Middle White or Large Black
2 large onions
6 sweetly tart cooking apples of the sort that don't collapse, or 6 large Coxes
6 fresh bay leaves
plenty of coarse sea salt and freshly ground black pepper
300–570ml/½–1 pint good dry cider such as Julian Temperley's Kingston Black from the Somerset Cider Brandy Company (01460 240782)
cooking water from your vegetables

Preheat the oven to 200°C/400°F/Gas 6. Peel and slice the onions thinly and place them on the bottom of a roasting tin. Sit the chined loin on the top, then sprinkle a goodly amount of salt over the top and some black pepper, and rub them in with your fingers. The joint will take 1½ hours to cook and a further 15 minutes or so to rest on your carving board, under foil and a tea towel.

Half an hour before the end of cooking time, rigorously core your apples – you do not want to find toenaily bits – and tuck a bay leaf into the top of each hole. Score a line through the skin around the circumference of each apple with the point of a sharp knife, and place them upright in the roasting tin with the meat. Baste them with the meat juices and a good splosh of the cider and cook for the meat's final 30 minutes. The apples may burst, but you are not looking for cosmetic perfection here; the flavour and texture are all.

Keep the apples hot while you slice the crackling horizontally off the joint in one piece, leaving as much of the fat as you can attached to the joint. Place the sheet of crackling under a hot grill and wait until it is molten brittle before returning it to the top of the meat. Do not cover the meat again or the crackling will sog.

Stir the meat juices and caramelized onion together in the roasting tin over a high flame, add the rest of the cider and, when it is bubbling, some water from whatever vegetables you have cooked. Reduce for a few minutes, then strain the gravy through a sieve into a large jug standing in the sink, before pouring it into gravy jugs.

ROAST CHICKEN
WITH A SWEETCORN AND GINGER STUFFING

It did make me slightly uneasy, stuffing a chicken with its daily diet of maize, and its own liver, but I promise you, this is one of the best stuffings ever; the ginger lifts it from ordinary to sublime. Do not add herbs, it would dull the pure flavours.

Serves 6 with leftovers

1 organic corn-fed chicken, mine weighed 3 and a bit kg/just under 7lb
1 onion, sliced
olive oil and butter
1 onion, peeled and chopped
2 celery stalks, with the leaves, chopped
5cm/2in fresh ginger, peeled and very finely chopped
the liver of the bird
2 corn cobs, cooked and the kernels stripped from the cob
a handful of breadcrumbs
1 egg, beaten
salt and black pepper

Preheat the oven to 200°C/400°F/Gas 6. Heat a film of olive oil and a knob of butter in a frying pan and add the chopped onion and celery. Stir to coat, then add the ginger, and cook until palely softened. Throw in the liver, chopped into seven or eight pieces, and cook for a further couple of minutes, until still very pink. Remove from the heat and add the corn, seasoning, a scant handful of breadcrumbs and the beaten egg, and amalgamate. Spoon it into the fowl's bottom, pressing it down well. Secure with a cocktail stick.

Put your sliced onion on the bottom of the roasting tin, then lay the chicken on its side on top. Season and slather with a bit of olive oil. Cook for 30 minutes a side, then sit the chicken breast up, sprinkle over some coarse sea salt, and cook for a final 30 minutes. Remove and leave to rest for 15–20 minutes under foil. Accompany with the usual roast potatoes, parsnips and other vegetables and gravy. I think bread sauce is not quite right with this, but I wouldn't dare not make it for the children.

BREAD SAUCE

I like bread sauce with some texture and find that some types of white breadcrumbs can make it a bit slimy. I prefer this method, with bits of onion, to the more usual one of putting in a whole onion spiked with cloves and removing it at the end of the cooking time.

Serves 6

1.2 litres/2 pints milk
1 onion, finely chopped
grating of nutmeg
1 bay leaf
black pepper
3 cloves
fresh wholemeal
  breadcrumbs
2 tbsp cream (optional)

Pour the milk into a saucepan and add the finely chopped onion. Add a good grating of nutmeg, a bay leaf, some black pepper, the cloves and enough fresh wholemeal breadcrumbs to not quite absorb the milk at first. Bring very slowly to simmering point, then stir and simmer for 45 minutes, adding more nutmeg and milk if needed. If you like, add a couple of tablespoons of cream at the end, although I don't think this is necessary. Remove the bay leaf and the cloves if you can find them, season to taste and serve hot.

THE BEST ROAST POTATOES AND PARSNIPS

3 small potatoes per person
1 small parsnip per person

Preheat the oven to 200°C/400°F/Gas 6. Peel the vegetables. Bring them to the boil in just enough water to cover and simmer for five minutes or until beginning to feel less like bullets. Drain the cooking water into a jug and use it for cooking other vegetables or for the gravy later – the floury starch from the potatoes is a natural thickener.

Put a couple of tablespoons of beef dripping, goose or duck fat, or fat from pork if you are cooking pork, in a roasting tin and heat to smoking point – about three or four minutes in a hot oven. Olive oil will do if you have none of the above. Remove the tin from the oven and sloosh the potatoes into it all around the edges of the tin where it is hottest. Put the parsnips in the middle. Turn the vegetables so they are coated in fat, then ruffle up the potatoes with a fork so they look slightly ploughed. Cook at the top of the hot oven, turning every 20 minutes or so. If the parsnips cook too quickly, put them in with the meat lower down in the oven. Potatoes can take anything from 40 minutes to an hour to crisp up well on all sides, so keep watching. Drain off the fat when you are ready to serve them.

GRAVY

Gravy. An emotive word. I remember as a child going to endless Sunday lunches with my parents and being appalled at the underfilled gravy jugs, the floury taste, the phoney gravy boats, the cooks who thought a teaspoon of bread sauce was an 'ample sufficiency' and didn't understand the concept of a lake of gravy. And the importance of having enough left to make your shepherd's or cottage pie with on Monday. Flour is out of fashion, but is bound to be revived at a later date. Meanwhile, these are my golden rules – making a surfeit should go without saying.

onions, peeled and sliced
water from parboiling
    potatoes
wine
seasoning

Roast your joint on a layer of peeled, sliced onions. The meaty juices will mingle with them, the onions will exude their flavour and juice in turn, and caramelize to a dark, crunchy, almost charred intensity. You have begun.

When you have laid your meat to rest on the carving board, whack the heat up, and put the roasting tin on top of the stove. Add a good splosh of whatever wine you happen to have open and let it seethe for a minute or two to burn off the alcohol. Take the potato water that you saved in a jug when you parboiled your potatoes and parsnips before roasting, and add it a little at a time, including the gorgeous, gluey, starchy bits at the bottom. These will help to thicken the gravy slightly without resorting to cornflour. You can add any other vegetable water as well if you need, as you stir like crazy to release the oniony morsels from their sticking places. They will colour the gravy a rich, burnished mahogany, so forget the horrors of fake browning.

Add more wine and seasoning to taste. Try Madeira or port with beef, really good cider with pork, white wine with chicken or Marsala with veal. Remember to add the blood that has leaked into the carving tray to the gravy before you put it into your jug, or into a French dégraisseur that leaves the fat at the top as you pour. It's as simple as that.

ROAST WILD DUCK

Allow one duck per brace of people. I have always cooked wild duck very simply, roasting at a high temperature, resting, and using the juices as the main ingredient for any sauce. Apricots are a brilliant foil for the stuffing, particularly the little dried Hunza ones from Afghanistan. Apples and celery also work well, as do sharper berries like red and blackcurrants, or a sharp midwinter Seville orange in the sauce. You can use bitter marmalade instead.

Serves 4

2 wild ducks
1 onion, sliced
butter
parsley, marjoram
lemon juice
salt and pepper

Preheat the oven to 220°C/425°F/Gas 7. For a rare bird, place the duck breast side up on a layer of sliced onion in a roasting tin. Add its liver mashed together with a lump of butter, some parsley, marjoram, salt, pepper and lemon juice. Roast for 25 minutes, then check with a skewer. The juices should run pink, but the bird should not feel resistant. Rest for a few minutes.

BRAISED ENDIVES

A simple, but unusual vegetable dish. Delicious with roast meat.

Serves 4

4–8 heads of chicory
   (Belgian endive)
olive oil
1 lemon
salt, pepper

Lay the heads of chicory in an earthenware or similar baking dish. Dribble over some olive oil and season. Cover and cook in a moderate oven, 160°C/325°F/Gas 3, for one hour. Squeeze the lemon over the chicory, return it to the oven for 30 minutes, then serve straight from the baking dish with the juices.

TARTE TATIN

Had the Tatin sisters from the Hotel Terminus Tatin near Orleans been able to patent this wonderful variation on the simple theme of a tart, with its caramelized sweet apples, they would have become as rich as they are now legendary. Don't imagine it is difficult to flip a tatin. I cook mine in a frying pan with oven-proof handles, but Le Creuset makes a lovely enamel tatin dish.

Serves 6–8

85g/3oz vanilla caster sugar
55g/2oz unsalted butter
8–10 crisp, well-flavoured
    eating apples (I prefer
    Coxes)
lemon juice

Puff pastry
170g/6oz plain flour
170g/6oz unsalted butter
(or use shop-bought puff
    pastry made with butter)

Preheat the oven to 180°C/350°F/Gas 4. Make the pastry and chill it in the fridge while you prepare the apples

Put the sugar in a heavy-bottomed frying pan or enamel tatin dish and heat it gently, keeping a beady eye on it. You want it to melt to a mahogany brown liquid without burning. Don't stir it, just shake the pan a little so it melts evenly. Switch off the heat and add half the butter in tiny bits – it will fizz and froth. Swirl the caramel up the sides of the pan.

Peel and slice all the apples into quarters, but keep back one half. Core them all. Squeeze a little lemon juice over them to prevent them discolouring. Pack a wheel of apples back to back around the edge of the pan, then another wheel inside it, and place the half apple, cut side up, in the centre. Dot with the remaining butter.

Roll out a circle of pastry just bigger than the diameter of the frying pan, put it over your rolling pin and lay it like a blanket over the apples, tucking the edges down into the pan like bedclothes.

Bake in the centre of the oven for 25–30 minutes. Leave to cool for 10 minutes before flipping out on a large plate with enough depth to house the black juicy moat of caramelized appley butter. Serve warm with crème fraîche laced with a little Somerset cider brandy or Calvados.

LEMON MERINGUE PIE

This is one of the first puddings I learned to cook. My grandmother's cook, Rhoda, steely grey hair in a taut bun, and maroon-flowered dress worn nearly down to her black, old maid's shoes, had the lightest touch that pastry ever saw. She always made this when my brother Daniel and I went to stay at Upper Parrock, our grandparents' beautiful medieval hilltop house in East Sussex. And she always judged it right. The gloopy lemon filling was never too sweet, never too cornfloured, and the top rose cloud-like, stepped, a breath of weightless meringue with that final, brittle brown top that a spoon had to crunch through before meeting the gooey middle and the smooth, tart lemon. The addition of a few crushed cardamom seeds to the lemon filling robs the pudding of its nursery status, but is well worth the experimentation.

Serves 6

23cm/9 inch shortcrust
   pastry case, chilled
beaten egg white, for brushing

Lemon filling
grated zest and juice of
   3 organic lemons
45g/1½oz cornflour
290ml/10fl oz water
3 large egg yolks
85g/3oz vanilla caster sugar
55g/2oz unsalted butter,
   cut into small pieces

Meringue
3 large egg whites
110g/4oz vanilla caster sugar

Preheat the oven to 190°C/375°F/Gas 5. Bake the pastry blind for 15 minutes, then remove the beans, brush the pastry with beaten egg white, and return to the oven for five minutes. Remove the pastry case from the oven and turn the heat down to 180°C/350°F/Gas 4.

For the filling, put the lemon zest and juice in the top of a double boiler. Add the cornflour and whisk in with two tablespoons of the water until you have a smooth paste. Bring the remaining water to the boil, add to the lemon mixture and keep whisking over simmering water until the mixture is thick and bubbling. Remove from the heat and whisk in the egg yolks, sugar and butter. Leave to cool slightly while you make the meringue.

Whisk the egg whites until stiff, scatter in one-third of the sugar, and whisk again until stiff. Fold in another third of the sugar with a metal spoon. Spread the lemon mixture over the pastry. Pile the meringue on top and sprinkle it with the remaining sugar. Bake for 15–20 minutes. Allow to cool slightly, then turn out. Best served with thin cream.

TRIFLE

This is no mere trifle. It is wondrously rich, fruity and full of hidden depths. Sheer hedonism and the perfect ending for a leisurely Sunday lunch.

Serves 6

5 macaroons
240ml/8fl oz white wine
4–6 tbsp raspberry liqueur
570ml/1 pint organic double cream
290ml/10fl oz milk
2 eggs and 2 yolks
1 tbsp sifted cornflour
vanilla caster sugar to taste
340g/12oz raw raspberries
icing sugar to taste
5 ripe peaches
juice of a lemon

Put five macaroons into a large glass bowl and pour over 120ml/4fl oz of the white wine and two or three tablespoons of raspberry liqueur.

Bring the milk and 290ml/10fl oz of the double cream to scalding point and pour them over the two eggs and two yolks, which you have beaten with the sifted cornflour. Return to the pan and whisk until thickened. Add vanilla caster sugar to taste and pour over the macaroons.

Purée the raw raspberries in a food processor, sieve and add icing sugar to taste. Pour this mixture over the cooled custard. Scald five peaches, skin and slice them, then place them on top of the raspberries.

Put the lemon juice and the rest of the white wine and raspberry liqueur into a bowl and stir in 30g/1oz sugar until dissolved. Taste for sweetness. Pour over the remaining double cream and beat with a wire whisk until thickened but not stiff. The mixture will have a lovely peachy blush to it. Spread over the custard and fruit in the glass bowl.

SUMMER PUDDING
WITH DEVON RASPBERRY LIQUEUR

I happen to believe that Elizabeth David and Jane Grigson got it right, the best summer pudding is made with raspberries and redcurrants only – about 4:1 rasps to reds.

Serves 6

675g/1½lb raspberries
200g/7oz redcurrants
110g/4oz vanilla caster sugar
1–2 tbsp raspberry liqueur
white bread cut into slices,
  the crusts removed

Put the raspberries and redcurrants in a heavy pot with the vanilla caster sugar. Heat gently and briefly until the fruit begins to bleed and the sugar is dissolved. No more than three or four minutes, the fruit must not lose its shape or cook.

Line a pudding basin with slices of day-old good white bread. There should be no gaps.

With a slotted spoon, pile in the fruit, leaving some of the juice in the pot. Sprinkle a tablespoon or two of raspberry liqueur over the pudding before finishing with a top layer of bread.

Cover with a plate that just fits, weight it, and put the basin in the fridge overnight. Turn it out just before you serve it on to a not completely flat plate, and pour over the rest of the juice, to which you've added more raspberry liqueur to taste. You should still pass round the bottle too!

BAKED ALMOND PUDDING
WITH APRICOT AND ALMOND JAM

This almond pudding has intimations of both Yorkshire curd and Bakewell tarts. You can plop the mixture inside a pastry crust if you are looking for something more heavyweight than a gloriously custardy, flourless sponge.

Serves 6–8

110g/4oz unsalted butter
225g/8oz almonds, preferably Valencia, carefully ground in a Magimix
a few drops Culpeper's bitter almond oil
4 large eggs, preferably organic
2 tbsp Oloroso sherry
zest and juice of half a lemon
110g/4oz vanilla caster sugar
500ml/18fl oz single cream or half cream/half Channel Islands milk
225g/8oz good-quality apricot jam

Heat the oven to 190°C/375°F/Gas 5. Melt the butter in a small pan. Pour it into a large bowl in which you have gently whisked all the other ingredients, except the jam, and whisk until they are amalgamated and the butter has been absorbed.

Grease a shallow pie dish with butter. Melt the jam very gently with a tablespoon of water until runny, then pour it into the dish. Pour over the pudding mixture, and set aside until you are ready to bake. The pudding takes between 30 and 45 minutes to cook, depending on the depth and circumference of the dish, but should have a distinct wobble in the centre when you remove it from the oven, and will carry on cooking. The top should be golden and slightly crusted.

Eat warm with clotted or pouring cream.

CHOCOLATE ST EMILION

This has nothing to do with the Elizabeth David one. This is much lighter and nicer. I found a recipe for something called Hungarian Chocolate on the back of an England's Glory matchbox. It needed jazzing up, and I wondered how I could get this mixture to make not a soufflé or a mousse, but something that would stand up in a glass. Gradually I arrived at what we thought was perfection. It is named after the little macaroons that St Emilion is famous for.

Serves 8

225g/8oz Menier chocolate
1 tbsp instant coffee
120ml/4fl oz water
4 eggs
3–4 large macaroons
40ml/1½fl oz brandy

Melt the chocolate in the water with the coffee. Separate the eggs, whisk the yolks, and add them to the chocolate at room temperature, mixing them in well. Crumble the macaroons roughly, sprinkle them with brandy, and mash with a fork. Whisk the egg whites stiffly and fold lightly, but thoroughly, into the chocolate mixture which should still be warm. Layer in glasses with the macaroon mixture.

STEAMED LEMON CURD PUDDING

I made one with lemon curd, and another with lime curd and a couple of ounces less sugar. Which was better? I can't say, the ointment-thick lake of curd spilling around the tangy pudding was equally as divine, just different. Eschew cream, for once – the sauce is rich enough. I used Thursday Cottage curds, available in good supermarkets and delis.

Serves 6

170g/6oz caster sugar
110g/4oz butter
2 eggs
juice and rind of 2 lemons
110g/4oz flour
1 tsp baking powder
a bit of milk to slacken
1 × 310g/11oz jar Thursday
  Cottage lemon curd

Cream the sugar and butter together thoroughly, then beat in the eggs. Add the juice and rind of the lemons, then sprinkle over the sifted flour and baking powder. Add a bit of milk to slacken to a dropping consistency, but don't let the mixture become sloppy.

Scrape the lemon curd from the jar into the bottom of your pudding basin, a snap-on lidded plastic one is fine if you don't want to cover and tie an old-fashioned pudding basin. Spoon the pudding mixture over the curd, cover, set on a trivet in a large pan, and pour boiling water to come half way up the sides of the basin. Simmer for about 1½ hours before turning out on to a large dish; remember there will be a lake of sauce.

CHOCOLATE AND RASPBERRY PUDDING CAKE
WITH CHOCOLATE GANACHE

This is a magical cake, which you can make without the raspberries if you are of a purist chocoholic bent, or simply don't agree with chocolate and fruit, which some don't. You can make the cake well in advance if you want — it will keep for a week in a tin — and then add your ganache. This cake is flourless, but moist with freshly ground almonds.

serves 8–10

4 organic eggs, separated, plus one whole egg
170g/6oz vanilla caster sugar
225g/8oz best bitter chocolate, minimum 70% cocoa solids, I use Green and Black's
140g/5oz blanched almonds, freshly ground
1 heaped tsp ground coffee
200g/7oz fresh raspberries

Ganache
225g/8oz dark chocolate
120ml/4fl oz double cream

Preheat the oven to 170°C/325°F/Gas 3. Whisk the egg yolks and egg together with half the sugar, until pale and doubled in volume. Melt the chocolate in a double saucepan. Whisk the egg whites, adding the sugar a bit at a time, until they are at the satiny, soft peak stage. Add half of the egg whites to the egg and sugar mixture, folding them in gently. Add the chocolate and the rest of the whites, folding as you go. Then do the same with the almonds and coffee. Last of all, add the raspberries, which need folding in with extreme gentleness so that they don't break up.

Scrape the mixture into a greased and floured 20cm/8in springform tin, with a circle of greased greaseproof paper laid on its base, and bake for 30 minutes. Then turn the oven off and leave the cake in for another 15 minutes or until a skewer comes out clean from the centre. Remove from the oven and leave to cool in the tin.

Scald the cream in a small pan, remove from the heat and stir in the broken up chocolate. Cover the cake with the ganache and leave to cool.

GUARDS' PUDDING

Known as steamed strawberry pudding by my children. Use a really good strawberry jam, clotted with whole strawberries, and if you want to be profligate, you can heat the contents of a second pot of jam to pour over pudding before serving.

Serves 6

170g/6oz wholemeal
  breadcrumbs
30g/1oz self-raising flour
85g/3oz vanilla caster sugar
1 pot best strawberry jam,
  full of whole strawberries
3 eggs
110g/4oz melted butter
1 tsp bicarbonate of soda

Grease a 1.2 litre/2 pint pudding basin or plastic equivalent thoroughly. Mix the breadcrumbs together with the sifted flour and sugar in a large bowl. Melt the jam gently and pour it into the bowl at the same time as the whisked eggs and melted butter. Stir together. Dissolve the bicarb in a little bit of water, and stir it into the pudding.

Pour into the pudding basin, and seal with pleated foil and string, or with the snap-on lid if you're using a plastic bowl. Place the pudding on a trivet, then pour boiling water to come halfway up the sides of the pudding basin. Cover with a lid and simmer for two hours.

Turn out, and serve with thick cream.

STRAWBERRIES AND CREAM

June means strawberries. Not the hideous, tasteless, acidic Elsantas, which have become a ubiquitous apology for the sweet, small, older varieties, but deep, dark, crimson, seedy strawberries picked warm from the sun. They don't need to be showered in sugar — just eat them with Jersey cream, stiff clotted cream or even a drop of aged balsamic vinegar to enhance the sweet and the sour. You can turn them into an Eton Mess with gooey shards of meringue and whipped cream, fold them into scented syllabubs, perch them on a tart or crush them into fools and ice cream.

Strawberries
double cream, Jersey
  if possible

Meringues
6 egg whites
500g/1lb 2oz caster sugar
flaked toasted almonds

Wash and hull the strawberries. Whip the cream until stiff, then pile layers of cream and strawberries into little individual bowls or glasses. To make Eton Mess, spoon in some broken up meringues.

OVERNIGHT MERINGUES

Preheat the oven to 150°C/300°F/Gas 2. Cover a large tray with non-stick baking parchment. Over a simmering pan of water, place a bowl with six egg whites and the caster sugar. Stir until the sugar has dissolved and the mixture is very warm. Beat with an electric mixer until thick and cool, then spoon large mounds on to the tray, three across and three down. Lightly sprinkle with flaked toasted almonds. Place the tray in the oven, turn off the heat, and leave overnight. The outside will be hard but the inside wonderfully gooey.

INDEX

A

almonds
Almond & Orange Florentines 75
Almond Macaroon Cake 84
Almond Macaroons 112
Baked Almond Pudding with Apricot & Almond Jam 135
Polenta, Almond & Lemon Cake 81
Quince & Pralinéed Almond Ice Cream 115
anchovies, Bagna Cauda 13
apples
Kirkham's Lancashire Cheese & Apple Tart 61
Roast Chined Loin of Pork with Baked Apples & Cider Gravy 124
Somerset Apple Cake 74
Tarte Tatin 131
apricots, Daube of Pork with Apricots 97
asparagus
Asparagus, Fennel & Red Pepper Salad 54
Cold Poached Salmon or Sea Trout with Griddled Asparagus & Green Mayonnaise 92
Aubergine, Feta & Mint Salad 52
aubergines, Ratatouille 90
avocados, Chilled Crab, Cucumber & Avocado Salad 120

B

Bagna Cauda 13
beans
Broad Beans with Preserved Lemon, Coriander & Spanish Paprika 57
Leg of Lamb Braised Slowly with Haricot Beans 122
Pork Hock & Bean Casserole 28
beef
Lasagne al Forno 18
Oxtail Stewed with Grapes 30
steak 103-4
Steak with Béarnaise 104
biscuits
Almond & Orange Florentines 75
Almond Macaroons 112
Chocolate Cookies 76
Ginger Biscuits 75
Bloody Mary, Home-Made 118

bread 36-8
Brown Soda Bread 42
Malted Grain Loaf 38-9
Pain Perdu or Poor Knights of Windsor with Jam Sauce 46
Pan Bagnat 62
Parmesan Grissini 89
Potato & Porcini Focaccia 51
White Loaf 40-1

C

cabbage, Stuffed Cabbage in the Troo Style 17
cakes
Almond Macaroon Cake 84
Caramel & Chocolate Fudge Cake 110
Chocolate Brownies 78
Chocolate & Hazelnut Cake 80
Chocolate & Raspberry Pudding Cake with Chocolate Ganache 138
Drenched Ginger & Lemon Cake 82
Orange-Scented Ricotta Cake 114
Parkin 79
Pineapple & Walnut Upside-down Cake 108
Polenta, Almond & Lemon Cake 81
Rich Chocolate Chip & Hazelnut Brownies 78
Somerset Apple Cake 74
Spiced Fruit Loaf 83
Strawberry Genoise 109
carrots
Moroccan Carrot Salad 54
Chicken Stewed with Carrots, Red Onions & Moroccan Spices 101
cheese
Aubergine, Feta & Mint Salad 52
Cheese & Thyme Scones 66
Cos Lettuce with Cashel Blue & Cream Dressing 69
Innes Buttons with Hazelnuts 12
Kirkham's Lancashire Cheese & Apple Tart 61
Layered Pancakes with Tomato Sauce 14
Orange-Scented Ricotta Cake 114
Parmesan Grissini 89
Tomato Chilli Jam with Goat's Cheese & Bruschetta 70

Tomatoes Baked with Olives, Mustard & Gruyère 55
Watercress, Pear & Roquefort Salad with Toasted Sesame Seeds 50
Winter Pasticcio 20
chicken
Chicken Savoyarde 98
Chicken Soup 68
Chicken Stewed with Carrots, Red Onions & Moroccan Spices 101
Coq au Vin 100
Roast Chicken with Sweetcorn & Ginger Stuffing 126
chicken livers, Spiced Chicken Livers 12
chocolate
Chocolate Brownies 78
Chocolate Cookies 76
Chocolate Ganache 138
Chocolate & Hazelnut Cake 80
Chocolate & Raspberry Pudding Cake with Chocolate Ganache 138
Chocolate St Emilion 136
Mousse au Chocolat 32
Rich Chocolate Chip & Hazelnut Brownies 78
White Chocolate Tart with Raspberries 33

D

duck
Honey-Blackened Duck Legs 29
Roast Wild Duck 130

E

endives, Braised Endives 130

F

fennel
Asparagus, Fennel & Red Pepper Salad 54
Pork Fillet en Papillote with Dijon, Fennel & Black Olives 28
fish
cod
Baked Cod, with Romesco Sauce & Greek Potatoes 22
Cod Charmoula 23
eel, Crêpes Parmentier with Smoked Eel, Crispy Bacon & Horseradish 60

haddock, Smoked Haddock Soufflé 94
salmon
Cold Poached Salmon with Griddled Asparagus & Green Mayonnaise 92
Salmon Fishcakes with Crème Fraîche Tartare 24
Smoke-Roasted Salmon, Watercress & Horseradish Sandwich 50
trout, Cold Poached Sea Trout with Griddled Asparagus & Green Mayonnaise 92
tuna, Fresh Tuna Sauce (Vitello Tonnato) 96
Turbot with Sauce Vierge 95
see also seafood
fruit juices 46

G

ginger
Drenched Ginger & Lemon Cake 82
Ginger Biscuits 75
Roast Chicken with a Sweetcorn & Ginger Stuffing 126
gooseberries
Gooseberry Fool 112
Gooseberry Muffins 43
Granola 44
Gravy 124, 129

I

ice cream
Quince & Pralinéed Almond 115
Vanilla 111

J

jam
Banana Jam 42
Tomato Chilli Jam with Goat's Cheese & Bruschetta 70
Juices 46

L

lamb
Breast of Lamb cooked in the Daube Style 26
Lamb Shanks Braised with Balsamic Vinegar & White Wine 102
Leg of Lamb Braised Slowly with Haricot Beans 122
Leeks Vinaigrette 88

lemons
  Broad Beans with Preserved
    Lemon, Coriander &
    Spanish Paprika 57
  Drenched Ginger & Lemon
    Cake 82
  Lemon Meringue Pie 132
  Polenta, Almond & Lemon
    Cake 81
  Steamed Lemon Curd
    Pudding 137

M
meringues 140
muffins
  Gooseberry Muffins 43
  Raspberry Muffins 43
mushrooms, Potato & Porcini
  Focaccia 51

N
nuts
  Bazargan or Cracked Wheat &
    Nut Salad 58
  Chocolate & Hazelnut Cake
    80
  Innes Buttons with Hazelnuts
    12
  Pineapple & Walnut Upside-
    down Cake 108
  Rich Chocolate Chip &
    Hazelnut Brownies 78
  Romesco Sauce 22

O
oranges
  Almond & Orange
    Florentines 75
  Orange-Scented Ricotta
    Cake 114
Oxtail Stewed with Grapes 30

P
Pan Bagnat 62
pancakes
  Crêpes Parmentier with
    Smoked Eel, Crispy Bacon &
    Horseradish 12
  Layered Pancakes with Pesto
    Sauce 16
  Layered Pancakes with Tomato
    Sauce 14
parsnips, Best Roast Potatoes &
  Parsnips 128
pasta
  Lasagne al Forno 18
  Pasta Puttanesca 19
  Winter Pasticcio 20

pastry
  Kirkham's Lancashire Cheese
    & Apple Tart 61
  Lemon Meringue Pie 132
  Tarte Tatin 131
peaches, Instant Nellie Melba
  Syllabub 106
peas, Minted Pea Purée 91
peppers 10
  Asparagus, Fennel & Red
    Pepper Salad 54
  Ratatouille 90
  Sicilian Peppers 10
Pineapple & Walnut Upside-
  down Cake 108
Plum & Rhubarb Compote 44
pork
  Daube of Pork with Apricots
    97
  Pork Fillet en Papillote with
    Dijon, Fennel & Black
    Olives 28
  Pork Hock & Bean Casserole
    28
  Roast Boned Leg of Pork
    with a Spiced Orange Rub &
    Orange Sweet Potatoes 123
  Roast Chined Loin of Pork
    with Baked Apples & Cider
    Gravy 124
potatoes
  Best Roast Potatoes & Parsnips
    128
  Potato & Porcini Focaccia 51
  Tortilla Española 56
puddings
  Baked Almond Pudding with
    Apricot & Almond Jam 135
  Chocolate & Raspberry
    Pudding Cake with
    Chocolate Ganache 138
  Chocolate St Emilion 136
  Gooseberry Fool 112
  Guard's Pudding 139
  Instant Nellie Melba Syllabub
    106
  Lemon Meringue Pie 132
  Mousse au Chocolat 32
  Pineapple & Walnut Upside-
    down Cake 108
  Steamed Lemon Curd
    Pudding 137
  Strawberries & Cream 140
  Strawberry Genoise 109
  Summer Pudding with Devon
    Raspberry Liqueur 134
  Tarte Tatin 131
  Trifle 133

pumpkin, Roasted Pumpkin &
  Coconut Soup with Thai
  Spices 64

Q
Quince & Pralinéed Almond Ice
  Cream 115

R
raspberries
  Chocolate & Raspberry
    Pudding Cake with
    Chocolate Ganache 138
  Instant Nellie Melba Syllabub
    106
  Raspberry Muffins 43
  Summer Pudding with Devon
    Raspberry Liqueur 134
  Trifle 133
  White Chocolate Tart with
    Raspberries 33
Ratatouille 90
redcurrants, Summer Pudding
  with Devon Raspberry
  Liqueur 134
rhubarb, Plum & Rhubarb
  Compote 44

S
salads
  Asparagus, Fennel & Red
    Pepper Salad 54
  Aubergine, Feta & Mint Salad
    52
  Bazargan or Cracked Wheat &
    Nut Salad 58
  Broad Beans with Preserved
    Lemon, Coriander &
    Spanish Paprika 57
  Chilled Crab, Cucumber &
    Avocado Salad 120
  Cos Lettuce with Cashel Blue
    & a Cream Dressing 69
  Moroccan Carrot Salad with
    Garlic & Coriander 54
  Pan Bagnat 62
  Watercress, Pear & Roquefort
    Salad with Toasted Sesame
    Seeds 50
sauces
  Bagna Cauda 13
  Béarnaise Sauce 104
  Bechamel Sauce 14
  Bread Sauce 14
  for Chicken Savoyarde 98
  Cream Dressing 69
  Crème Fraîche Tartare 25
  Fresh Tuna Sauce 96

Green Herb Mayonnaise 93
  Jam Sauce 46
  Pesto Sauce 16
  Romesco Sauce 22
  Sauce Vierge 95
  Tomato Sauce 14
sausages, Stuffed Cabbage in the
  Troo Style 17
scones, Cheese & Thyme Scones
  66
seafood
  Chilled Crab, Cucumber &
    Avocado Salad 120
  Scallops with Minted Pea
    Purée 91
  see also fish
soups
  Chicken Soup 68
  Easy Roast Cherry Tomato
    Soup 66
  Roasted Pumpkin & Coconut
    Soup with Thai Spices 64
Steak 103-5
strawberries
  Strawberries & Cream 140
  Strawberry Genoise 109
sweetcorn, Roast Chicken with
  Sweetcorn & Ginger Stuffing
  126
syllabub, Instant Nellie Melba
  Syllabub 106

T
tomatoes
  Easy Roast Cherry Tomato
    Soup 66
  Home-Made Bloody Mary 118
  Layered Pancakes with Tomato
    Sauce 14
  Ratatouille 90
  Tomato Chilli Jam with Goat's
    Cheese & Bruschetta 70
  Tomatoes Baked with Olives,
    Mustard & Gruyère 55
  Tortilla Española 56

V
veal, Vitello Tonnato with Green
  Olives 96

W
watercress
  Watercress, Pear & Roquefort
    Salad with Toasted Sesame
    Seeds 50
  Smoke-Roasted Salmon,
    Watercress & Horseradish
    Sandwich 50

First published in the United Kingdom in 2004 by Weidenfeld & Nicolson

This edition first published in 2005 by Weidenfeld & Nicolson

Photographs by David Loftus

A CIP catalogue record for this book is available from the British Library

ISBN 0 297 84393 1

Printed in Italy

Weidenfeld & Nicolson

The Orion Publishing Group Ltd
Orion House
5 Upper Saint Martin's Lane
London WC2H 9EA

Design director David Rowley
Editorial director Susan Haynes
Designed by Nigel Soper and David Rowley
Edited by Jinny Johnson
Proofread by Gwen Rigby
Index by Elizabeth Wiggans